The Entrepreneur's Toolbox

How to Succeed in Your Small Business
While Manifesting Your Destiny

© by Krysta Gibson

Copyright 2007 by Krysta Gibson
All Rights Reserved

ISBN 978-1-4303-2382-2

No part of this may be copied in any manner
without the explicit written permission
of Krysta Gibson.

The author may be contacted at krysta@krystagibson.com
www.krystagibson.com

Krysta Gibson is creator of
the CD program
Embrace Your Day, Love Your Life
For more information: www.krystagibson.com

She the publisher of New Spirit Journal, a monthly publication that helps people create abundance in their relationships, finances, health, career, and spiritual life. For more information: www.newspiritjournal.com

What people are saying about
The Entrepreneur's Toolbox

"The work and expertise the author has put into this marvelous book is astounding! She has her finger on the pulse of the spiritually-minded entrepreneur! I highly recommend taking this class if you are wanting valuable insights in starting or expanding your own business."
Norma Menzies
Founder
"The Bluebird of Happiness Club for Everyone"
www.bluebirdofhappiness.org
www.normamenzies.com

"The Entreprenuer's Toolbox will be a great help to people whether they are starting out in their businesses or if they need a boost to get their businesses back on track. I too have been through all the ups and downs of being an entrepreneur, and Krysta's stories and warnings are so true. They will assist those going through that for the first time. It is so easy to think you are the only one having those experiences. And it is easy to panic when things are not flowing as expected...only to find that that is the natural flow after all. The material is timely, topical and sound. Great job!"
Mary Lee LaBay
Author and Catalyst for Personal Growth
www.maryleelabay.com

"Although I have been a shaman and healer for 25 years and I have been director of the Family of Light Healing Centre for 10 years now, I found The Entrepreneur's Tool Box to be very insightful, and easy to read. It offered help in understanding why one should operate a holistic practice with spiritual marketing tools, I would recommend this course/ebook to anyone serious about operating a holistic business."
Charles Lightwalker, Ph.D.
Metis Shaman
www.familyoflight.com

"Krysta Gibson has drawn on her years of experience in the business world to create a wonderful book, The Entrepreneur's Toolbox, which guides small business owners to the pinnacle of success. Unlike anything else I have read she clearly explains how business success and spirituality are not mutually exclusive, but can and should be fully integrated. If the reader follows Krysta's instructions they will indeed be not only successful, but happier in their business pursuits. This is a must-read book for both experienced and novice business people."
Ron Kalvin
Clinical Hypnotherapist
kalvins@earthlink.net

"As I read The Entrepreneur's Toolbox, I became awed by the scope of this work and the lifetime of learning that preceded it. It's everything anyone would need or want before, during, and even after owning a business. Most of the programs that are available today focus on building a business, but Krysta covered some other very important areas, such as the possibility of having to get a job and what to do when your business becomes so successful you want to franchise it. Separating the sections into weeks was perfect because it gave me just the right amount of time to do the exercises and to absorb all the information.

"I especially loved the client profile exercise, in which the target market is identified. I've been told to do this before, and have done it to some extent, but Krysta's exercise took me much farther and opened up deeper awareness for me about my market. Then she gave suggestions about how to use this information. Information is of no value unless it can be put to use, and then it becomes priceless. I highly recommend this book!"
Kathy Wilson
Life Purpose Coach and Spiritual Teacher
www.aninnerjourney.com

"If you are self-employed or would like to be, and want your business to be personally meaningful, creative, and a successful service to others, don't hesitate to take Krysta Gibson's Entrepreneur's Toolbox course. Left and right brain, heart, soul, and mind will be fed, guided, and inspired with Krysta's wit and wisdom, and down-to-earth practicality. Step by step, week by week, breath by breath, let the Toolbox be your personal business trainer."
Hriman (Terry McGilloway)
Minister and Former CPA
Ananda Center for Self-Realization
www.anandaseattle.org

"The Entrepreneur's Toolbox by Krysta Gibson is filled with common sense, practical tools that work and wonderful messages of inspiration. It covers a wide variety of topics that are not covered by previous books and gives a heads-up on issues that many people don't ever consider when starting a business. Whether you're already in business or just starting a business this book is an invaluable spiritual tool and guide; easy to read and incorporate."
John Jennings
School of Light
johnlight@aol.com

"Starting a new business can be very exciting, yet it can also be overwhelming, trying to set up all that needs to be done. I found The Entrepreneurs Toolbox extremely helpful with do-able steps and usable information to get your business off to a flying start. Even if you've been in business for awhile, you'll find the info quite valuable."
Lori Aletha, of the NW Psychic Fairs and
Director of The NW Center of Enlightenment
www.lorialetha.com

"Are you ready for a practical, hands-on, commonsense book that explains how to follow your bliss and grow your business? Good news! You just found that book! In a very clear and entertaining style, Krysta shares marvelous techniques to help entrepreneurs glide their craft over the sometimes choppy waters of the business world. Following Krysta's advice has made an enormous difference in my business and has significantly increased my income. Her suggestions and techniques are invaluable, and there is no better cheering squad. No matter your experience level, I urge anyone in business to read The Entrepreneur's Toolbox!"
Rhonda Dicksion
Indigo Dog Design
www.indigodog.com

"I have recently changed careers and started a new business, so I am saturated with self help books about starting a business. However, I can say that if I only had room for one book in my bookshelf, this would be the one I would keep. It is a fabulous wealth of information written in a manner that makes you know that you can do anything you need to do to create a business that feeds your soul. This course is totally practical and very readable. I didn't follow the instructions, but instead read it in two sittings. Now I am going to go back and actually "take the course" as it was designed to be taken and actually complete the exercises. It will be fun to look back six months from now and see how the business is growing, and without a written record I wouldn't have a yardstick to measure my progress. Other books have suggested this approach, but this is the first book that actually explained the reasoning behind completing the exercises, which made me want to take my time and fill in the blanks.

"Krysta mentioned money ideas that had never occurred to me. Her examples are perfect because they actually apply! The sources and resources are current, available and right on point.

"I recommend this Toolbox to anyone wanting a business that is spirit-based but who also wants mainstream recognition (they aren't mutually exclusive) because this course gives a way to live your life and play in your business instead of living your business and playing only in your life. It instills in a business owner that it is okay to be a success, and who doesn't want that! This will be a wonderful resource because it will always give me new ideas on how to succeed in my business as I (and my business) grow. It is a Must Read!"
Kathie Brodie
Consulting Hypnotist
www.HarvestoftheHeart.com

"I found everything in The Entrepreneur's Toolbox to be very clearly explained and in the order needed. Unlike some lightworkers, my path guided me to become educated in business first. I have an MBA and years of experience "working for others." I was blessed this past year with the opportunity to take my business experience and "book-learning" and fulfill a long-burning desire for more spiritual and service based work. Our store has been a dream manifested, but as you know, being a business owner can cause "balance" issues. Your toolbox has all the steps a "university" class would offer, but also offers the holistic and spiritual overtones that make it a unique and necessary opportunity for anyone in the spiritual or services community who is struggling, or doesn't know how to get started. I especially appreciated the bonus articles. Thank you (and my angels) for the constant reminders to step back, breathe, and meditate!"
Peace & Gratitude,
Angela Atwell, Spirit Tree Gifts
spirittree@rockisland.com

"As a Metaphysical stand-up comic and motivational speaker, I was somewhat cowed by what appeared to be the Herculean task of finding my own relevant audiences for whom what I do would matter. With the support of Krysta Gibson's system, I streamlined my approach, effectively 'doing less and accomplishing more.'

"After reading The Entrepreneur's Toolbox, measurable results began to occur immediately for me, in alignment with my highest vision for myself: a film director I admire asked to work with me, other people on the speaking circuit and several speaker's bureaus approached me. My back-of-the-room sales were just handled. Now I have the wherewithal to write my book!

"If the sub-atomic field responds to the mind of (wo)man, eavesdropping on our thoughts, we are powerful beyond measure. Krysta's toolbox works in concert with this awe-inspiring Universal 'YESNESS,' and I now know that my career's going to go how I say it's going to go."
Vanda Mikoloski
http://www.vanda.us

"When you have the right set of tools for the job, the work itself just flows. And the right set of tools for starting or building a business are now at hand. The Entrepreneur's Toolbox by Krysta Gibson really delivers the goods. You even get inspiration, wit and wisdom as part of the package. Krysta reveals that smart business and a spiritual orientation are the ideal mix for success."
James Conti,
East West Bookshop
Mountain View, California

"Not only is The Entrepreneur's Toolbox full of practical, easy-to-follow information for a start-up business, I found it an invaluable source of inspiration for those already in business. As a holistic practitioner, it is crucial to have such useful advice in a spirit-centered practice. Krysta's words are motivating as they are inspiring. I encourage everyone to read this book!"
Ami Karnosh, MS
Certified Nutritionist
www.karmanutrition.com

"The Entrepreneur's Toolbox is a must for anyone in business! It is a comprehensive and extremely informative resource as well as being highly practical and relevant to today's business issues. While it is geared at the holistic practitioner, its applicability and relevance is to all small business enterprises. Even after nine years of operating as a sole proprietor I found new and meaningful options and strategies to enhance my business direction. Thank you, Krysta, for sharing your invaluable skills and knowledge in this great business package!"
Bente Hansen, Healing Arts Practitioner
Author of The New World of Self-Healing
www.dynamicenergyhealing.net
www.imagroupmembers.com/bentehansen

*Dedicated to brave entrepreneurs everywhere:
you are the backbone of our society!*

Contents

Introduction...11

Week One
Your vision..15
Your mission statement...16
Your business plan...17
The Someday-Maybe Box..18
Goals and to-do lists..19

Week Two
You as a legal entity..21
Taxes..23
Other legal information...24
Bookkeeping and accounting..25
Hiring staff..26
Policies and procedures..27
Supervising employees...28
Handling problem employees and terminations......................29

Week Three
What is this thing called marketing?..31
Do you know who your clients are?..32
Surveys..34
What to do with your client profile..34
Your "elevator speech"..35
Focus!..36
Tracking results..37

Week Four
Consistency..39
Marketing tools...41
Writing your marketing plan..47
Creating a market...48
Tips about your website...49

Week Five
Putting it all together...52
Use all of your tools..52
Minding your manners...54
Small goals, small steps...55
Money! Money! Money!..55
Delegate..57

Breaking through your resistances...57
You're succeeding: now what?..58
It looks like you're failing: now what?...59
Selling your business..61
Franchising your business...63
Resources..65
Course evaluation..68

Appendix..70
Letting there be peace in your business..70
Advertising is like going fishing...71
What to do when discouragement sets in.....................................73
Flowing with the go of your business...74
How to tell if advertising dollars are being well-spent.....................76
Marketing ideas that don't cost a lot of money.............................77
Minding your manners..80
Riding the tides of change..82
Success...84

Introduction

The Entrepreneur's Toolbox is designed especially for people who are in business for themselves who also consciously walk a spiritual path of some sort. Because of this, the course has a mix of "worldly" business tools and more intuitive/spiritual ones. Some people equate being spiritual with being religious. Actually, the various religions are "brands" of spirituality. Many very spiritual people are not religious at all. This book can be used by anyone of any religion or spiritual belief.

If you purchased this book, it is because you are operating your business according to holistic principles. All this really means is that you see your business as more than a way to make a living (although it is certainly that); you also see it as your service, your way to help others in one way or another. Your business is part of your path in life.

I think that being called to operate a small business in combination with a spiritual practice or base is one of the most interesting, satisfying, and challenging vocations there can be. As an entrepreneur you are able to chart your own course and take responsibility for the outcomes. No matter what happens with your business, it is always a fascinating journey for your soul, mind, and body.

The reason I decided to write this book is because there are many people who have tremendous gifts to offer without having the benefit of some solid business knowledge. Too often I have seen people start their businesses with great enthusiasm only to run into roadblocks caused by lack of business experience. It is my hope that this course can fill in some of the blanks for people so that they can live their heart's desires.

Having said this, I want to be clear that I don't claim to be some sort of business guru. What I am is a business person who has learned how to combine business and holistic principles in such as way as to be materially comfortable while following my bliss and living my beliefs. In other words, I am in business for myself, providing a service to others, and I am happy.

My Background

My business background spans over 30 years and includes a variety of businesses: insurance, employment consulting and headhunting, machine shop industry, skin care consulting, psychological counseling, newspaper publishing, writing, management of a retirement community with a multi-million dollar budget, retail, tarot consultant, and operating a non-profit senior center.

I have not worked in the large corporate environment and I have tended to specialize in smaller companies and have owned several myself. I have walked the entire cycle of starting a business with no capital, operating it for eleven years, and then selling it. I have used a second mortgage to buy a "sick" business I thought I could rejuvenate only to have the economy go flat two months later. And I owned a retail business long enough (one year) to know this is not my bliss – and to give me great admiration for people who operate small retail shops!

In other words, I have done a lot of different things that have given me an incredible base of knowledge and experiences to draw on. I have seen (and done) some things that work and some that don't. What I offer to you in this course are some ideas and techniques that have worked for me and for other entrepreneurs I have had the pleasure to work with. I know a lot, but I don't claim to know everything! Take what suits you and leave the rest.

If you already know some of the information I present, consider it a refresher course! For me, I know how important it has been to learn the same information from different teachers so it would really stick with me. It has also been invaluable for me to learn similar information from different people because each teacher puts their own flavor and seasonings into the stew!

The Course

I have taken the areas clients ask me about most often and compiled the information most commonly requested. Business is a fascinating topic and there are countless books that address many different areas. You are encouraged to do some online or library research for more in-depth information. At the end of the course I give a bibliography of some of my favorite books, classes and internet sites.

The course is divided into five weeks. Each covers certain topics and also includes some exercises that will help you work with the information presented. It is very important that you do the exercises if you want to get the most out of this course. Having said that, this is your course – take what you want and leave the rest! You don't have to do the course in the order presented. It is fine to skip around according to your interests and needs.

It is a good idea to get a notebook where you can keep your exercises when they are done. One of the early reviewers of this course, Ron Kalvin, said: "I would suggest they *need* to get a notebook. They should organize this with all of the material they will develop from your book. Then the book should be used and referred to. This book is their roadmap to success and it has the energy of their business success within it."

I have tried to keep your time involvement to a few hours each week. How long it takes will depend on how long it takes you to read each lesson and do the exercises. You don't need to rush: you can work in your own timeframe.

Quotes

You'll find quotes sprinkled throughout the course. These are some I have found to be helpful so wanted to share them with you. I have found them in various places and give credit to the author, although I was not able to reference the particular place the quote was found. When it is known, I have given the person's website information.

Business Consultations

Some readers have expressed an interest in having consultations with me. If you want a business consultation with me, information about that can be found on my website www.krystagibson.com.

Survey

At the end of the course you will have the opportunity to fill out a survey about the course, letting me know what did or did not work for you.

Weekly emails

I offer a free weekly email by subscription. It is called The Entrepreneur's Toolbox. If you are not signed up for that and would like to, please email me at krysta@krystagibson.com. I also have a mailing list for people who are interested in the newspaper I publish, New Spirit Journal. If you want to be on that list, email me at krysta@newspiritjournal.com.

The Entrepreneur's Toolbox

Week One

This first week we are going to focus on your vision, mission statement, business plan and goals. We hear and use this word *vision* a lot. What does it mean as it is applied to our business? Your vision is the big picture of what you want to accomplish. It is you letting your imagination run wild as to what you want to accomplish through your business. Vision is what tells us where we are going and it puts the punch and the why into what we do. Some people's vision is to heal the planet. For others it is world peace. For still others, it is to make beautiful music or art or literature.

Before you can effectively start or operate a business, it is vitally important to know your vision. Why are you in business? Some people will answer, "To make money; to pay the rent; to get rich." Although an exchange of money has to take place in order for you to be in business, usually making money is not the vision of a business – at least not for a business that is operating according to holistic principles. Money is what happens while you're busy providing service!

"Where there is no vision the people perish." — Proverbs 29:18

"The one thing worse than not being able to see is having no vision."
— Helen Keller

"For a person to carry on a successful business he or she must have imagination. He must see things in a vision, a dream of the whole thing." —Charles M. Schwab

Some people can come up with their vision immediately and don't have to spend a lot of time on this step. Even if you think you know what your vision is, write it down. It is amazing how many people don't take their vision and put it into the third dimension where we live: the world of matter. You want your business to manifest in the world of matter so it is only logical that you need to get your vision out of your head and heart and onto paper or at least into your computer. I adore using computers and I own and use a handheld Treo. *And* I still write tons of things by hand because there is something very intimate about putting pen to paper.

"Goals in writing are dreams with deadlines."
— Brian Tracy www.briantracy.com

If you are not clear on your vision, start asking, "How may I serve?" Look at your talents, your interests, your background. Look out at the world and see what it is looking for and needs that you might be able to provide. Then stay open to ideas that pop into your head.

Sometimes people have a vision of providing some type of service but the world (or at least the world where they live) does not want or need that service. For example, if you live in the desert it is not likely that there is a big need for a ski lift. And if you live in the snowy mountains, there is probably not a big outcry for a golf course.

When coming up with your vision for your business, do your homework and be sure that what you want to offer has an audience that wants it – or that you feel you can create the audience or need. We will discuss creating need or desire in a different lesson.

Sample visions:
My vision is to heal the planet.
My vision is to create world peace.
My vision is to help people eat healthy food.
My vision is to teach spiritual principles.

Stop now and do exercise #1
My Vision is: (Write in your notebook)

Your Mission Statement

The next step is to ask yourself how you are going to do this. What do you plan to do to create world peace or to heal the planet? This step is going to give you your mission statement in one sentence. Your mission statement is broad and big. This is not the step for details.

Sample Mission Statements:
I help to heal the planet by providing naturopathic services.
I create world peace by providing a store where people can buy books and music that help them feel peaceful.
I create world peace by giving massages.
I help people eat healthy food by operating an organic farm.
I teach spiritual principles by giving classes and workshops in my local area.

Stop now and do exercise #2
My mission statement is: (Write in your notebook)

Write out your mission statement by hand or on your computer so it is nice and big. Make several copies. Put them where you can see them frequently. Be sure you have a copy in your datebook or PDA where you will see it. The reason for this step is that everything you do in your business from this day forward has to fit within this mission statement. If it doesn't, you need to question why you are doing it. Either you need to amend your mission statement or you need to put that idea in your Someday-Maybe Box (more on that in a minute).

"I find it fascinating that most people plan their vacation with better care than they do their lives. Perhaps that is because escape is easier than change." — *Jim Rohn*
www.jimrohn.com

Your Business Plan

There are few better ways to clear a room of business people than to say those two words: *Business Plan!* This is especially true in our community, where we involve our intuition and visioning techniques in deciding how to operate our businesses. I have some good news for you and it is this: you don't have to be afraid of business plans anymore *and* a business plan will actually help your intuitive skills, not hurt them.

There are at least two kinds of business plans. One is the kind you write for a bank or other investor when you are asking for a loan. These tend to be very detailed and involve a lot of financial calculations as well as speculation about future performance. Although this kind of plan is a great idea even if you are not seeking a loan, it is not the sort I am discussing here.

The plan I am talking about is made with broader strokes and is used as a map or barometer for decision-making. It is based on how you intend to carry out the mission statement you wrote in the last exercise. Your plan will be a broad outline of how you intend to make your big vision a reality.

"People with goals succeed because they know where they're going."
— *Earl Nightingale*
— *www.nightingaleconant.com*

Let's say your mission statement is to help bring peace to the planet. Here are some ideas for your business plan.

"I help people feel more peaceful by giving them massages."
"I assist people in feeling more peaceful by giving talks and seminars in the Puget Sound area."
"My website gives ways for people to find their inner peace."
"The oils and stones I sell to my clients help them create more peace in their lives."

Come up with four to five ways you intend to make your big vision a reality. Remember, you are using broad brushstrokes, not filling in all the details. When you are done with this you should have a one-page, very simple description of what your business does. This becomes the backbone of everything you do.

Stop now and do exercise #3:
My Business Plan: (Write in your notebook)

Using this sort of a business plan allows you to truly focus on what you want your business to be, and helps you do only those things that will support your vision. This does not mean you can't amend the plan or add to it. However, if you really found your "sweet spot" with the first step, you will find that the additional ideas truly belong in the Someday-Maybe category and by being able to file them away for the future your business will be stronger and will help you live your vision by being more focused!

"An average person with average talent, ambition and education, can outstrip the most brilliant genius in our society if that person has clear, focused goals." — Brian Tracy

"By recording your dreams and goals on paper, you set in motion the process of becoming the person you most want to be."
— Mark Victor Hansen, www.markvictorhansen.com

The Someday-Maybe Box

You are most likely a very creative person who has an interest in many different things. I'll bet sometimes your head wants to burst with all the ideas you have and can see yourself doing. Although it is wonderful to be full of so many ways to serve and help, the danger is that by trying to do too much too soon, you will lose your focus and not do anything very well. It is difficult to turn away from a really good idea but if you don't stay focused, you will not be able to produce much of anything.

Get a box or blank book or create a file on your computer. Call it your "Someday-Maybe Box." Any time you have an idea to do something, hold it up against your mission statement and your business plan. If it does not fit right now, the idea goes into this box. Once a quarter, four times a year, you can pull this box out and look at what is in here. If it fits your current plan and you want to do it, pull it out and go for it. If it doesn't, back into the box it goes.

Doing this satisfies your need to be creative while also helping you to focus on the tasks at hand. It is amazing how things that go into this box find their way into your life – or not! Giving these ideas a place to be and to germinate - or to die - saves you a tremendous amount of energy and helps you stay focused.

Stop now and do exercise #4:
Create your Someday-Maybe Box

"Goals that are not written down are just wishes." — Anonymous

"You'll never achieve your dreams if they don't become goals." —Anonymous

"Obstacles are what you see when you take your eyes off your goals."
— Anonymous

Goals and To-do Lists

Now that you have your vision, mission statement, and business plan done, you are ready for the step that most people do first. Now you will see why goals and to-do lists are pretty meaningless and don't work for a lot of people unless they have done the first three steps.

Your goals are based on your business plan. Take each item of your business plan. Put it at the top of a piece of paper. Now, write down all the things you have to do in order to make that part of your business plan a reality. Here is an example:

"I help people feel more peaceful by giving them massages."

Goals
Get my massage license.
Practice giving massages so I am good at it.
Find a place to give massages
Build a client list.
…and so on.

The to-do list is based on the goals and this is the most changeable of this whole process. You will do a to-do list daily so that you stay on-task with your goals and business plan.

To do list
Research massage schools in my area. Will I need to move?
Decide on what school I want to attend.
Apply to the school.
…and so on.

As each thing on the to-do list is accomplished it gets crossed off and the next thing is added.

Exercise #5
Create your current goal list and a to-do list

Get a piece of paper for each of the items on your business plan and write one item on each piece of paper. Now take each one and write down all the things you need to do in order to have each of those items come about. Once you have done that (and this is fluid – you will be adding and subtracting to this list as you go along); create a to-do list for at least one of the items. Carry this to-do list with you and do at least one thing from it each day, more if you can.

"Go as far as you can see, and when you get there you will see farther."
—*Orison Swett Marden*

"To solve a problem or to reach a goal you don't need to know all the answers in advance. But you must have a clear idea of the problem or the goal you want to reach."
—*W. Clement Stone*

Summation of Week One

If you have done the exercises for this week, you are now very clear on what you want to do and where you are headed. Congratulations! You now stand heads and shoulders above most people you know!

Do not do these exercises and then forget them. That is why I suggested you get a journal or notebook. Your vision, mission statement, business plan, goals, and to-do lists are living, breathing organisms. They are an integral part of who you are and why you are here at this time. Hold them close and dear to your heart. Be ready to jot down ideas as they come to you because they will. Once you have done this work you have invited the assistance of many beings who want to see you succeed.

Carry a notebook and pen or a tape recorder with you. Always be able to write down or record a thought when it comes to you. Thoughts are like hummingbirds. They come to you and buzz around you and then are gone as quickly as they came. Ideas are constantly floating around in the atmosphere; be sure you get your share!

I hope you have enjoyed your first lesson. In the next lesson we will talk about some very basic business things such as legal, accounting, taxes, licenses, bank accounts, staffing, etc. Even if you have been in business for awhile, this can be a good review for you.

Week Two

Now that you have your vision and plan and goals, let's be sure you are operating legally and intelligently! It is not uncommon for people to forge ahead without having the proper business licenses in place, without any sort of accounting system, and without a handle on such things as paying taxes. We tend to be a right-brain bunch and don't always want to do our left-brain chores.

You will be much more successful and happy if you go ahead and play by the world's rules. Some of the rules might seem pretty silly to you but they are there for a reason and many of them ensure the common good. In order to have time to spend on your vision, it is better to get your business-house in order so you don't have to waste precious energy worrying about whether or not the taxman or city official is going to come knocking at your door and shut you down.

If you have been in business for awhile some of this will be repetition, but maybe you can give it a glance to see if you are missing anything. If you are new to business, this can help get you off on the right foot!

You As a Legal Entity

In order to be in business, our society has set up various legal structures and you need to choose which one you want to be. A lot of people skip this step because they feel intimidated by it. The purpose of this section of the course is to un-intimidate you!

My Disclaimer: read this!

I am not a lawyer. I am not an accountant. I am not telling you what to do. I am giving you some information and I do not claim that this is all the information you need to make a decision. This is very basic. I suggest that you do more homework to learn about these various possibilities. I also suggest you contact an attorney if you have legal questions. I suggest you contact an accountant if you have accounting questions.

The way you set up your business will determine many things, not the least of which is how many rules you have to follow, how you will pay taxes, etc. In most states you also have to register your business. Although the forms are fairly similar in different states, there are variations. Because I live and work in Washington State, I will be using information from that state. If you are in another state or country, do some research and find out how all of this applies to you. Use Google: doing business in (your state) or country.

The following is taken directly from the Washington State website:
http://access.wa.gov/business/start.aspx

> **Types of business formats**
> **Taken from the Washington State Website Above**

"You may operate your business under any one of several organizational structures. Each type of structure has certain advantages and disadvantages that should be considered. You should contact an attorney, accountant, financial advisor, banker, or other business or legal advisor to determine which form is most suitable for you.

*A **Sole Proprietorship** is one individual or married couple in business alone. Sole proprietorships are the most common form of business structure. This type of business is simple to form and operate, and may enjoy greater flexibility of management and fewer legal controls. However, the business owner is personally liable for all debts incurred by the business.*

*A **General Partnership** is composed of two or more persons (usually not a married couple) who agree to contribute money, labor, and/or skill to a business. Each partner shares the profits, losses, and management of the business, and each partner is personally and equally liable for debts of the partnership. Formal terms of the partnership are usually contained in a written partnership agreement.*

*A **Limited Partnership** is composed of one or more general partners and one or more limited partners. The general partners manage the business and share full in its profits and losses. Limited partners share in the profits of the business, but their losses are limited to the extent of their investment. Limited partners are usually not involved in the day-to-day operations of the business.*

*A **Limited Liability Partnership (LLP)** is similar to a General Partnership except that normally a partner does not have personal liability for the negligence of another partner. This business structure is used most commonly by professionals such as accountants and lawyers.*

*A **Corporation** is a more complex business structure. As a chartered legal entity, a corporation has certain rights, privileges, and liabilities beyond those of an individual. Doing business as a corporation may yield tax or financial benefits, but these can be offset by other considerations, such as increased licensing fees or decreased personal control. Corporations may be formed for profit or nonprofit purposes.*

*The **Limited Liability Company (LLC)** and the LLP are the newest forms of business structure in Washington. An LLC or LLP is formed by one or more individuals or entities through a special written agreement. The agreement details the organization of the LLC or LLP, including: provisions for management, assignability of interests, and distribution of profits or losses. Limited liability companies and limited liability* *partnerships are permitted to engage in any lawful, for profit business or activity other than banking or insurance."*

There is a lot more good information there and I suggest you spend some time at that site this week so you can make the correct decisions for your business. Even if you are actively in business and are set up, there is still some good information there. This site tells you about the various legal steps you need to take to operate a business. These steps vary greatly depending on what you are doing. Go to the website (or a similar one for your state or country) and see what applies to you.

"A non-doer is very often a critic – that is, someone who sits back and watches doers, and then waxes philosophically about how the doers are doing. It's easy to be a critic, but being a doer requires effort, risk, and change." —Dr. Wayne W. Dyer
www.drwaynedyer.com

"Finish each day and be done with it. You have done what you could. Some blunders and absurdities no doubt crept in; forget them as soon as you can. Tomorrow is a new day; begin it well and serenely and with too high a spirit to be encumbered with your old nonsense."
—Ralph Waldo Emerson

A Word About Taxes

Okay, two words about taxes: pay them! You have a vision and a dream. Don't ruin it by avoiding paying your taxes. I know there are people who are fighting the IRS system of taxation and feel it is not fair or legal. Good for them. If this is their life's work, let them go for it. If you are a store owner or a healer and then decide to take on the IRS what will happen is you won't be able to be an effective healer or store owner. You must decide what is more important to you: dealing with the IRS or operating your business.

Sometimes people get behind on filing their taxes and then get scared to file because they don't know what might happen to them. Years go by and it gets worse. Sometimes people let their tax situation keep them from opening business bank accounts and/or getting licenses because they are afraid of getting caught by the IRS. If this describes you, the best thing you can do is find a good accountant you can trust, go see them and tell them what sort of shape you are in tax-wise. He or she will help you sort through the mess and get your tax house back in order. Even if you owe taxes, most likely you will be able to set up a payment schedule.

You are not the first person in the world to have had this happen. A good accountant will not judge you for what has happened. He or she handles this sort of thing all the time and they know how to support you in the process. You will feel much better when you have it sorted out and handled!

A great way to avoid the problem in the first place is to set up a tax bank account. Put a certain percentage of your income into this account every month. You can ask your accountant what a good percentage figure would be for you. Then at the end of the year (or the quarter, if you pay taxes quarterly), you will have the money you need. This is also a great idea once you start hiring employees and have to pay payroll taxes. Just set up a separate account for those funds and they will be there when you need them.

Other Things You Need to Do

If you operate your business within city limits, you might need a city license. Contact the city where you will be conducting business to see what you need to do. Some counties require registration and licenses; contact the county in which you intend to do business and see what you need to do.

No matter the form your business takes, you will need an Employer Identification Number (EIN) from the federal government. Many people don't think they need to do this if they do not have staff, but you do if you intend to have any sort of business bank account and want to operate legally.

To get your EIN, go to:

http://www.gov-irs.com/main.php

If you are a professional of some kind such as a therapist, counselor, massage practitioner, etc.…you might have to have a particular license in order to operate a business. Consult with your state or country to find out what is required.

Exercise: Decide what sort of entity you are and get yourself set up and registered; get licenses, etc. If you have already done this, review your choices and be sure they are working for you. If not, seek counsel as to what sort of changes might be in order for you.

"Never mistake activity for achievement."
—John Wooden, www.johnwooden.com

"God put me on earth to accomplish a certain number of things.
Right now I am so far behind I will never die." —Anonymous

Bookkeeping and Accounting

Again, not a favorite subject for many of us but a necessary one! Here are the basics you need to know (remember my disclaimer: if you need the help of an accountant, go see an accountant!).

From day one (or from today if you are already in business and missed this step), keep your business and personal finances separate! You will need a separate bank account for your business so get one set up. The bank will want your EIN number and your state registration so have those in hand before you go to the bank.

Exercise #2: Set up a business bank account. If you already have your account set up, review it and be sure it is correct for your type of business. Also, see if you need a second account for any reason. If so, get one set up.

You will need to be able to keep track of your income and your expenditures. Depending on your business, you may need to be able to send invoices and/or give receipts. What works for many people is the Quickbooks accounting program. You can purchase it online or at most office supplies stores. It is well worth the investment. The program walks you through setting up your bookkeeping system and then keeps track of everything for you. At the end of the month, you can see how much money came in and what you spent. At the end of the year, you can print out reports to take to your accountant, which makes life much easier for both of you. There are other accounting programs out there. Do some research and choose one that fits your needs best.

If you don't want to use a computer system, purchase a ledger book from an office supply store and write down how much money you take in, when you spend it, and on what.

Keep receipts of everything you buy. Set up a filing system in categories you use: office supplies, gasoline, insurance, inventory, printing, etc. As you gather receipts, put them in the proper file. At the end of the year it will be very easy to gather up your receipts to be sure you declare everything you can on your taxes.

The sooner you have a system in place, the better. You will be much happier if you do this early on in the life of your business. It will save you a lot of time and energy that is better spent on your vision! If your business is complex, see an accountant who can help you get set up well before tax time rolls around!

Exercise #3: Set up your bookkeeping system and start using it. If you have this set up, review it and be sure it is working for you and that you are actually using it. Sometimes people set up such a system and then fail to use it. If this is you, get caught up and start using it!

Hiring Staff and Setting Procedures

Right now you might be in business by yourself and you might not plan on hiring staff. But in case you do, here is some information to help get you started. Before you hire each person, decide what you want them to do and what sort of skills you want them to possess. This is done through a job description. Here is what a job description might look like.

ABC Senior Center
Job Description: Driver

Position Function:
To safely transport the elderly or disabled under the business of the senior center.
Requirements:
High school diploma; valid commercial driver's license; one year's experience. Must be able to pass background and drug tests.
Responsibilities:
- Ensure the safety and comfort of all passengers transported by the center in a friendly and professional manner.
- Familiarize self with the vehicle, daily maintenance checks and report any repairs needed.
- Schedule vehicle for maintenance work as needed and for when schedule allows.
- Keep the vehicle clean on the inside and outside to ensure safety and a professional appearance.
- Make sure wireless phone is readily charged and working properly.
- Keep a daily maintenance log of mileage driven, and expenses incurred. Turn receipts and any paperwork into the administrative assistant.
- Maintain good communication between you and the center staff as issues and questions arise.
- Abide by all safety regulations, laws and ordinances while driving for the senior center.
- Report all accidents, including personal injury of self and/or passenger, to the director, regardless of whether there is apparent damage and/or injury.
- Report any traffic citations, accidents, and/or conviction or change in driver's license status, whether incurred during or outside of work for the center.
- Consent to annual motor vehicle record and criminal history checks.
- Consent to random urinalysis tests when requested.
- No tips can be accepted, although riders can donate to the center.

Hours of work: Varies according to center and/or participant schedule.
Supervised by: Program Director
Compensation: Wages range from $8.00 to $11.00/hour.

A good job description contains the title of the job, what sort of requirements must be met by an applicant to get the job, the function of the job, the duties, how many hours per week or month the job entails, who the employee will report to, and what sort of wage the employee can expect to make.

> *"All of us perform better and more willingly when we know why we're doing what we have been told or asked to do."* —Zig Ziglar
> www.ziglar.com

Writing the job description accomplishes a couple of things. First, it helps you gain clarity about the position. It helps you to know exactly the type of person you are looking for and will save you a lot of time when considering candidates for the job. Second, it helps you write a good ad for the position if you decide to advertise the opening. Third, it provides you with something to hand to candidates and it answers many of their questions. Be sure the new employee signs a copy for their employee file. Fourth, having a signed job description helps if there are ever any disagreements about the duties or expectations about the job. It helps when an employee says, "But you never told me I would be doing …" Pull out the signed job description and find out why they don't remember that part of the discussion!

Policies and Procedures

A lot of people don't make a policy and procedure manual because it seems to be a huge task they don't have time for. Trust me when I say that the time you will spend for *not* having procedures in place will be a lot more than the time it takes to write it in the first place. You will have certain issues you will need to cover for your particular kind of business, but here are some areas to get you started.

Days and hours of work.
Dress code, if any.
Behavior expected in the workplace.
Banned behavior in the workplace.
Policy regarding background or drug checks, if any.
Anti-discrimination policy.
Anti-harrassment policy.
Name the paid holidays, if any.
Vacation and sick policies; lunch and break policies.
Policies about notification when a person quits or is terminated.
Insurance policies.
What to do if an accident happens.
Emergency procedures.

This website gives a much more comprehensive list:

http://www.managementhelp.org/policies/policies/polslist.htm

This website from the same organization gives help as to writing an employee handbook:

http://www.managementhelp.org/policies/handbook/basics.htm

Supervising Employees

Book upon book has been written about how to manage or supervise people. It is an art, that is for sure. I love the book title, "Managing people is like herding cats!" I will give just a few basics here.

The number one rule is to treat your staff the way you want to be treated. A lot of bosses get into power trips with their staff and cause a lot of unnecessary heartache for themselves and others. Because you are operating your business from a spiritual base, you will attract a different sort of employee – I didn't say easier, I said "different."

"The best job goes to the person who can get it done without passing the buck or coming back with excuses." —Napoleon Hill, www.naphill.org

Because you are on your path, you will most likely attract others who are on their paths. This could mean a lot of karmic situations which are not always pleasant! The best advice I can give is to be very clear with your staff when you hire them. Have everything in writing. Let them know what is expected of them and let them know what they can expect from you. There are a lot of laws you have to abide by because you are an employer. Find out the regulations in your state and be ready to abide by them.

Create a fun place to work but also one where people take pride in a job well-done. Be ready to be a leader. You are the boss. This means you set the tone. Don't think that you can behave one way and then expect the staff to do the opposite. Your staff is an extension of you and the environment you are creating. Working with a staff that is well-trained, excited about what they do, and who enjoy one another (and you) is an almost blissful way to spend your day! Just don't forget that you are the boss.

Generally, the staff are not your personal friends. If they become personal friends this can open up an entirely different sort of working relationship. It could be good or it could create a huge challenge. Just remember: this is your business and everything you do and all the decisions you make will affect the business. Make all your staffing decisions with this in mind and you should be all right.

You will have turnover. You will be very fortunate to find people who will stay with you for years, especially if you are offering minimum wage, part-time work. Don't take it personally when someone leaves you. Of course you are sorry to lose someone you have trained and who is a big help in your business. But when it is their time to move on, let them do so gracefully and look forward to getting to know your next employee.

Handling Problem Employees and Terminations

Clarity is the most important thing to have when handling problem employees. The first time you have a problem with someone, start a diary on them. You can do this on paper or in your computer. Start documenting what they do or don't do and your response to the situation. If it is a serious issue, give them a written warning letter and have them sign it. Many times this is enough to get the person's attention and the problem goes away. If not, this documentation will help you if you do have to terminate their employment.

No one wants to be sued for unlawful termination. No one wants to pay excessive unemployment taxes for an employee who was not doing their job. Document. Document. Document. As they say in the healthcare field: if it isn't written down, it didn't happen!

Your employee handbook should spell out what happens if there are problems. It should say how many verbal warnings a person will get and how many written warnings they will get before being terminated. Make sure the person signs a form stating they have received the employee handbook so they cannot claim they didn't know the policies.

Praise your staff when they do a good job. Find ways to reward them. Look for what they do right rather than for what they do wrong. You know how good it feels to be appreciated; do the same thing for your staff. Appreciate them and let them know when they please you.

"Encouraged people achieve the best; dominated people achieve second best; neglected people achieve the least." —Anonymous

Exercise #5: Write a job description for your first employee, even if you don't expect to hire one right away. Perhaps you can write your own job description!

"The harder you fall, the higher you bounce." —Anonymous

"The person who wakes up and finds themselves famous hasn't been asleep!" —Anonymous

Week two is over now. I know this was a lot of left-brain information, but it was all necessary. We have covered a lot and you deserve a break. Go do something fun. Take a walk. Play with the dog. Watch a movie. Enjoy a cup of tea. Me? I am going to start a fire in the fireplace and have a cup of cocoa.

The next two weeks will be a lot more fun as we move into talking about marketing your business. One of my favorite sayings is this:

*"You can be the best healer in the world
but if people can't find you who will you heal?"*
—Krysta Gibson

Week Three

This course is going to get very exciting this week. You have your vision, business plan, goals, and to-do list done and you are keeping up with them as you grow and develop. You're a legal entity and have your bank accounts and bookkeeping set up. You are ready to hire staff when the time comes (if you haven't already) and you have your policies and procedures manual written or at least started. Now, let's get the world to know about you!

Far too often I have seen people set up great businesses or events and then have a less than desirable turnout. It is easy to fall into the trap of spending all your time and resources creating your business and then fail to market it. I think this happens because people don't understand the basics of marketing and they think it has to be complicated and expensive. It doesn't. This course is geared to the smaller business, so I am going to keep the information aimed at this level. Larger firms would get into a lot more technical and complicated formulas that are not necessary for smaller organizations.

"A stumble may prevent a fall." —English Proverb

"God gives every bird a worm, but he does not throw it into the nest."
—Swedish Proverb

What is This Thing Called Marketing?

In its simplest form, marketing is telling potential customers and clients about yourself in such a way that they will want to do business with you and/or refer others to you. We will be discussing this in lessons three and four. Many people confuse marketing and advertising and think they are the same thing. They aren't. Advertising is a form of marketing. We will be talking about this as well as about many other ways to market yourself.

Everything you do is marketing. Whether you are answering your telephone, sending an email, or putting a flyer out somewhere, you are marketing yourself. Your customers and potential customers are constantly evaluating you in one way or another. A simple thing like answering the telephone gruffly when you or your staff are in a hurry can make a customer decide to go somewhere else. This is especially true of receptionists and store clerks. When a customer is not greeted with warmth and enthusiasm, they don't want to do business with you. None of us is perfect and we all have days we would rather be anywhere than at work, but our basic manners in business are one of our chief marketing tools! We'll talk about manners later.

Whether it is the letter carrier making a delivery or a fellow professional who stops in unexpectedly, everyone is a referral source for you. If people get the impression that you are unfriendly, they are not very likely to pass your name along to potential clients. Marketing is happening all of the time whether or not you are aware of it!

> *"Success is simply a matter of luck. Ask any failure."*
> —Earl Nightingale

One of the biggest mistakes people make is spending hours and many dollars on marketing without taking the first important step. That step is to answer this question:

Do You Know Who Your Customers Are?

This might seem a silly question. Of course you know who your customers are! But, do you really? Can you pull out a piece of paper listing their attributes? Telling you where they shop? What they read? What they want from you? Where they live? What sort of work they do?

In other words, have you sat down and created a profile of your customer? Most entrepreneurs never do this. The successful ones do. Before you can even begin to think about crafting a marketing plan, you need to know who your clients or customers are.

Imagine going fishing without knowing if you were fishing in a lake or river or ocean. (This is catch-and-release, by the way!) Different fish live in different places, eat different food, sleep at different times. If the angler doesn't know what sort of fish he or she wants to catch, their success will be hit and miss.

The same is true with your business. You need to know who you are looking for before charging out into the world. Some people say they are looking for everyone and anybody. Not true. Not everyone wants or needs what you have to sell. You will be much more successful if you admit this, create a profile of your customer, and then tailor your marketing to find those people.

For instance, someone could present the world's best marketing of baby products to me. They would not make a single sale no matter how wonderful the marketing piece, their prices, location, or anything else. I am not going to buy baby products because I do not have a baby in my life. I don't even notice such information because it is not something with which I resonate.

> *"My success has allowed me to strike out with a higher class of women."*
> —Woody Allen

The time you spend on answering the question of who your clients are will come back to you multiplied many times. This simple act of defining your customers is the base of everything you will do in marketing. Skip this step and you can waste time and money that you won't get back.

If you don't know the profile of your customer off the top of your head, you will need to do some research. Look at successful businesses similar to yours and see who they are targeting and how they are doing it. One of the big secrets to successful marketing is called "market research." This can be complicated or simple. All this means is finding out about your customers, their needs and desires, and how your business might fit into their lives.

"Everybody's a self-made man; but only the successful ones are ever willing to admit it." —Anonymous

Exercise: Create a profile of your client

Answer the following questions in your notebook. If you can't answer them immediately, do some research until you can answer them. If the question does not relate to your business or product, skip it or write down that it doesn't matter.

1. Is your client male, female, or does your business appeal to both equally?

2. What age range does your client fall into?

3. Where does your client live?

4. Where does your client shop?

5. What sort of education does your customer have?

6. What income bracket is your customer in?

7. What profession are they in and what sort of position do they hold?

8. Is your customer new to your product/service or do they already use it?

9. What books and publications does your client read?

10. What sort of movies and television would they watch, if any?

11. Do your potential clients listen to the radio? If so, what time frame and what sort of stations (music or talk)?

12. Does your client use the internet? Email? Are they computer savvy? Does this matter to you?

13. Are they likely to listen to podcasts or own an iPod?

14. Do they ride the bus?

15. Describe their spiritual interests; do they belong to specific groups or churches, etc?

16. Describe their physical activities (yoga, running, jogging, etc.)

17. What does your customer want or need from you?

18. Do you provide what your customer wants/needs or can you?

20. What might cause a potential customer to use your product or services?

19. What might cause a potential customer not to use your product or services?

Surveys

If your business is already established and you want to grow, you have a wonderful opportunity to find out how to attract more clients your way. Conduct a survey of your current clients/customers. Find out more about them and their habits. This can give you an idea where to focus your marketing efforts. If you work with clients on the internet and have their email addresses, you can conduct online surveys using companies such as SurveyMonkey.com or Zooomerang.com. There are many others. Just use your search engine to look up online survey companies.

If your clients are not online, put together a simple survey that won't take more than a few minutes to fill out, and offer some sort of reward or discount to them for taking the time to answer your questions.

"Achievement seems to be connected with action. Successful men and women keep moving. They make mistakes, but they don't quit."
—Conrad Hilton

What Are You Going to Do with this Client Profile?

Your client profile tells you the sort of stores, publications, radio stations, and other areas, where you want to focus your marketing efforts.

For instance, if your business is geographically-based, such as a small corner grocer, you will want to put a lot of your marketing dollars into signage. Why? Because most of your customers will learn about you by driving or walking past your location, see you are in the neighborhood, and decide to stop in to see what you have to offer. You would also want to place your advertising dollars into local publications that are read by people close to your business. You would want to post flyers in other locations in your area where your customers might shop or visit: laundromats, libraries, pet shops, coffee shops. You might want to look at using a "door-hanging" service to take flyers around to the houses within a one-mile radius of the store (or hire teenagers to do this for you). Placing advertising in a publication that is distributed in a three-state area would be a waste of your marketing dollars.

What if you are a counselor or healer or massage practitioner? After you do your client survey, you will have your client profile. From that, you will have some idea of what sort of marketing strategy to put in place. What sort of information on a flyer, brochure, or website will appeal to these people? Where will you need to make the information available to them? Will they find you in publications? Bulletin boards? Radio shows? Word of mouth? The answer is probably yes to all of these. Where you decide to put your marketing dollars will depend on your budget, what sort of exposure you are comfortable with, and how large a geographic area you are covering.

When we get into specifics of marketing and your marketing plan, all of this will start coming together for you.

On a metaphysical level, you are not only drawing up a client or customer profile, you are also creating a pathway for those people to be drawn to your business. You can use this profile in your visualizations and goal-setting processes.

"You are not here merely to make a living. You are here in order to enable the world to live more amply, with greater vision, with a finer spirit of hope and achievement. You are here to enrich the world, and you impoverish yourself if you forget the errand." —
Woodrow Wilson

Your Elevator Speech

The term "elevator speech" is one that is starting to be used a lot. Having an elevator speech and knowing how to use it is a very useful marketing tool that can be used in many different situations. Here is what Wikepedia says about it:

*"An **elevator pitch** (or **elevator speech**) is a brief overview of an idea for a product, service, or project. The pitch is so called because it can be delivered in the time span of an elevator ride (say, thirty seconds or 100-150 words). The term is typically used in the context of an entrepreneur pitching an idea to a venture capitalist to receive funding. Venture capitalists often judge the quality of an idea and team on the basis of the quality of its elevator pitch, and will ask entrepreneurs for the elevator pitch so to quickly weed out bad ideas.*

"It is said that that many of the most important decisions made on the floor of the House or Senate are made 'in the spate of an elevator ride' as a staff aide whispers into a congressman or senator's ear while they head down to the floor to cast their vote.

"A variety of other people, including intrapreneurs (employees who act in an entrepreneurial way within an organization) project managers, salespeople, evangelists and job seekers commonly use elevator pitches to get their point across quickly."

An elevator speech is important because not only is it a terrific answer when people ask what you do, but the crafting of your speech will help you get very focused on exactly what you do and why you do it.

Exercise #2: Craft your elevator speech

Get out pen and paper or open a file on your computer. Answer these questions.

1. Who or what is your target market? You just created your client profile so this question should be easy to answer.

2. What problem or situation do they have that your company addresses?

3. What is unique about the solution you offer?

4. What action do you want them to take in relationship to you or your business?

Your speech should be no more than 150-200 words and should not take longer than two minutes, no longer than the time it would take to ride an elevator from the lobby to the third floor. It should also not use techno-babble and your grandmother as well as your children should be able to understand what you are saying.

Here is mine for this course:

I have a book called The Entrepreneur's Toolbox. It is for owners of small businesses who are really good at what they do but they want some help with things like marketing, planning, and other aspects of business. My book is arranged to be studied over a five-week period, is easy to use and to understand and addresses the basic issues faced by small businesses. Because my clients are busy people, they love being able to take the course in their own timeframe, whenever they want to, without having to drive somewhere after a long day's work. My course is specifically geared to people who believe in what are called holistic ideas, people who believe in approaching life and business with their bodies, minds, and spirits. Let me give you my card. Feel free to give it to anyone you think might be interested in The Entrepreneur's Toolbox.

After you craft your speech, give it to people you know and ask their opinion. Rewrite it and practice it until you can give it easily, without stumbling, as if it is second nature to you! The next time someone asks, "What do you do?" you will be able to answer the person in a complete way that also asks for a referral. Who knows, that person might be a future client!

Focus! Focus! Focus!

As you may have noticed, I am not a proponent of shotgun marketing. Although this can work for some businesses, it really isn't very effective for most small businesses. Shotgun marketing is where you place ads everywhere and anywhere that gives you a "deal," without consideration for your targeted client. In my opinion, you might as well fly over your city in a helicopter and drop flyers out the window. If you create a profile of your customer and then target your marketing efforts to those particular people, you will have more success in a shorter period of time for less cost. What business person doesn't want that?

"Hell, there are no rules here – we're trying to accomplish something."
— Thomas Alva Edison

Tracking Results

Ask your clients how they found out about you whenever you can and keep records of what they tell you. This is one way to find out what sort of return you are getting for your marketing dollar. Be careful, here, however. I have seen some people make poor decisions based on this data because it does not show the entire picture. We will talk more about this in next week's lesson. But, as an example, word of mouth is a very important source of business for all of us. I know people who don't do any other marketing except to rely on their current clients to tell others about them. This can work if you are very good at what you do, if you have been doing it long enough to have a lot of clients, and if you have a repeat business where you can build a returning client base. Yes, this is the chicken and egg thing! But how can word of mouth work for you when you are new to business?

I have also known people who quit advertising in a particular venue because they didn't have enough people saying they had seen their ad or flyer. Over the years I have learned that advertising works in many other ways than just having the person who saw the ad come to your business. Many times the person who saw the ad or flyer tells a friend about you (there is that word of mouth), the friend comes to see you; he or she says a friend referred them and you never know it was your ad that actually brought you the business. You think it was word of mouth! We'll talk more about this next week.

"Everyone is trying to accomplish something big, not realizing that life is made up of little things." — Frank Clark

End of Week Three

This was a lot to absorb and the exercises will probably take you a bit of time this week. This sets the groundwork for everything that follows, so please do the exercises, even if you have done them before! Next week we will talk about specific forms of marketing and your marketing plan.

The Entrepreneur's Toolbox

Week Four

This week we are going to make good use of the information you put together last week. If you are like most of the people who have taken this course, you were quite enlightened by the client/customer profile you came up with. I have heard some business people actually gasp when they understood that they had been watering down their marketing efforts by trying to lure people who were not suitable for their goods and services.

This week we are going to look at the wide variety of advertising and marketing possibilities that exist so you can devise your marketing plan – one you will actually use!

Before we do that, however, I want to make a very strong statement to you, one I hope you will take to heart because it is the basis of every successful marketing strategy. It is this.

> **Once you decide on a marketing plan or strategy, be consistent long enough to get results.**

There have been many times I have seen people decide to market their business in a particular way, start doing it, and then stop because they did not see immediate results. It is wonderful when our marketing produces immediate results – and sometimes, it does. However, it is not uncommon for a strategy to take time to work, especially for a newer business that is not very well known. Sometimes we need to readjust our plan and play with it for awhile before it begins to work for us. If we stop too soon, we will lose the benefits of the results that were beginning to happen for us. Your marketing mantra is: "Consistency, consistency, consistency!"

This does not mean that you don't change strategies that aren't working for you and it doesn't mean you don't experiment with a variety of ideas. You do. It means you give things a chance to work before you decide to make changes.

"Find a meaningful need and fill it better than anyone else."
–Anonymous

"As you climb the ladder of success, check occasionally to make sure it is leaning against the right wall." –Anonymous

Most people would agree that consistency is very important if we want to accomplish anything. From dieting and exercising to learning a new language, it is important to do something often enough and long enough to get results.

In business this can sometimes be a challenge. The entrepreneur decides on a product or service and starts providing it. When business doesn't show the immediate results desired, many people are tempted to change course right away. I saw this recently with a little consignment shop that opened not far from where I live.

The little store opened with a lot of flair and I heard many people talking about it and saying how much they loved shopping there. Three months later, there was an "Everything Must Go – Closing Sale" sign in front of the shop. Perhaps they should have saved their money and not opened in the first place!

In order to succeed in business in is important to decide on a course of action and stick with it long enough to see some results. How long? That really depends on the nature of the business, but a year would be the minimum for most. A year gives enough time to have traveled through the various cycles and seasons any business faces. It is long enough to see a trend in one direction or another.

I see this with advertising a lot. A person runs an ad once or twice, sometimes even three times. When they don't get the results they want, they stop advertising and do something else. I have been known to tell people to save their money if they are not willing to commit to an advertising program. It is sort of like getting in your car and heading to Portland and when you get to Olympia being upset because you aren't in Portland, turning around and coming back to Seattle!

Being consistent doesn't mean you can't try new things. It doesn't mean you can't experiment with how you provide your service or product. It does mean you make a commitment to your business with a "no matter what" attitude while being open to ideas and methods that come to you through your intuition.

"Saturate yourself with the idea of plenty, and the vibration of plenty will manifest in your affairs – plenty of love, plenty of health, plenty of true place opportunities, plenty of money, plenty of time, plenty of wisdom, plenty of fun, plenty of peace, plenty of joy, plenty of vitality, plenty of inspiration. Plenty-plenty-plenty!" –John Randolph Price www.quartus.org

Being in business for yourself is very much a dance with life where you can't always see what the next step or tune might be. There are many variables and factors to consider. What is important is to stay with the same partner long enough that you can learn when to lead, when to follow, and when to take a rest on the sidelines.

It is also true that sometimes our business is not working and it is time for us to let go and move on to something else. We can't be sure, however, unless we give the process enough time to work. It would be a pity to stop following our bliss just because we didn't give it enough time. Who knows, maybe you are just getting ready to manifest your heart's desire?

Take a look at the past six months. Have you been consistent in your efforts or has it been a hit and miss proposition? Are you committed to your business? How can you be more consistent so that you can see the fruits of your efforts more quickly and consistently? Have you given enough time for a particular strategy to work before deciding to change course?

Marketing Tools

Now for the fun! Here are some different marketing tools and ideas for you to consider. You might want to mark the ones you think suit your business most so you can revisit them once you start putting your marketing plan together.

Business Cards:

What do you think is the least expensive form of advertising? When I ask this question in my business classes, virtually 100% of the business people answer "word of mouth." Is that what you thought of right away? In my experience, word of mouth – although very important to any business – is not generally the least expensive form of advertising. Here's why.

When your business is new, you don't have customers yet so you don't have people talking about you to their friends and associates. It takes time to build a client or customer base. How long it takes to build that base and the amount of marketing and advertising you have to do in order to build it must be worked into the equation about how much word of mouth really costs you!

There are people who have been in business so long that they really can use word of mouth as their primary form of marketing. Usually this applies to people who provide personal services such as physicians, massage practitioners, healers, and so on. These professionals also have a limited amount of people they can see so filling up their practice with word of mouth can be a practical method to use.

So, without word of mouth, what is the least expensive form of advertising? Your business card! Designed properly and used consistently (never leave home without it), it is the least expensive form of advertising there is!

Your business card is not the place to skimp when it comes to the design. You want something that will stand out and something that represents you and your message. Too often, people open a file on their computer and crank out a card they think is pretty and start using it. That might work for some people, but I advise you to speak with a professional when you design a business card. You will be handing it out to just about everyone you meet so it needs to represent you well. Your business card should carry your energy so that when someone looks at it they will have a sense of you and your business.

You should always have your business card with you, in your pocket or purse and be able to produce it instantly. I have needed mine in the checkout line at a grocery store, in the pet store, and on the ferry. You never know when you will strike up a conversation with someone about your business and need to be able to produce your card. Be sure your contact information is complete and easy to read.

Business cards used to be expensive to print. Now you can get double-sided, color cards for about $100 per 1,000. This is too inexpensive to pass up!

> *"I have a wonderful business, in a wonderful way,*
> *I give wonderful service, for wonderful pay!"*
> *–Florence Scovel Shinn*
> *www.florencescovelshinn.wwwhubs.com/*

Your website

In today's world, you need to have a website. In years past, it was critical to have a brochure or other printed material to give to people. Today if you have to choose between a brochure or a website, go with the website. As with your business card, the website is not the place to skimp. It needs to represent you and what you do. If at all possible, have it designed by a professional. There are many people who call themselves web designers. Some are good and some are not. At the end of this lesson I am attaching some information for you about how to work with a web designer.

Once you have a website, be sure it is listed on your business card, at the end of every email you send, and on any other marketing materials you might have.

Brochure

Having a brochure that describes you and your services is optional. Not everyone has the sort of business that lends itself to a brochure. If you do decide to print a brochure, again I recommend using the services of a professional if at all possible.

Flyers

Depending on what you do, it might be important to use flyers to promote your services or your business. If you use flyers, keep them simple and don't overuse graphics or various typefaces.

Press Releases

Just about every area has a local newspaper of some sort. These smaller papers are usually looking for local news and ideas. Get the names and emails of newspapers and magazines that are published in your area. Find out who the editor and reporters are. Get their email addresses. When you offer an event or something of special interest, send them a press release about it. Do this on a regular basis so they get to know about you and what you do. Visit their offices and introduce yourself. Over time they will get to know you and they will consider you an expert on whatever it is you do. When the time comes that they have a question about your area of expertise, they will contact you. You might even get an article written about you in your local newspaper!

> *"Everything that you need, you already have. You are complete right now, you are a whole, total person, not an apprentice person on the way to someplace else. Your completeness must be understood by you and experienced in your thoughts as your own personal reality."*
> *–Wayne Dyer*

Writing articles

Some publications accept articles about a variety of topics. The newspaper I publish (www.newspiritjournal.com) is totally composed of articles written by local holistic practitioners and business people. Publications such as this one don't usually pay for articles, but they do offer a few words free at the end of the article that talks about who you are and what you do. Do some research in your area and see what sort of publications might be interested in your articles. If you are not a writer, look into taking some writing classes or have a friend help you.

Joining Groups/Community Involvement

Another important way you can market yourself is by getting involved in your local community. Are there are issues in your community that are important to you and that you would be willing to volunteer your help? Are there local charities such as the food bank, senior center, youth group, etc… that you could support with your time and/or money? This is a great way to be of service while also helping yourself get known in your community for whatever it is you are doing. People like to support others of like mind.

Becoming involved in your local Chamber of Commerce is a great way to network. There are starting to be local Holistic Chambers of Commerce as well so joining one of those is another great marketing tool. (In Washington state it is www.washingtonholisticchamber.org)

There are women's groups and men's groups. It seems there is a group for just about every profession you can think of. Make a list of as many groups as you can. You will need it later when it is time to write your marketing plan.

"We all have a natural ability to do at least one thing on a superstar level. When we locate what it is, and do it as though the quality of life depends on it, each of us becomes a superstar." –Arnold M. Patent
www.arnoldpatent.com

Start your own group

If you can't find a group that meets your needs, start your own! You can meet at restaurants or cafes or at your home. Most libraries will also let you hold meetings free as long as you don't charge an admission. Starting your own group has the advantage of your being able to set it up they way you want it to be. The downside is you have to organize it and stay on top of it. This can get time consuming. You have to weigh the advantages and disadvantages. Perhaps you can find a friend who wants to help you so all the work doesn't fall on your shoulders.

Professional speaking

There are a lot of groups and organizations who are always looking for interesting speakers: Chambers of Commerce, Kiwanis, Lions, Rotary Clubs, PTAs, etc… You could contact these groups in your area and get on their agendas to speak about your area of expertise. It is a great way to build your business and get yourself known in the community.

A word of caution: This will backfire if you are not a good speaker. Just because you enjoy being in front of people does not mean you are good at it. Record or video yourself giving a talk. Ask for feedback from a good – and honest – friend. If you are not a good speaker, join Toastmasters. This is a fabulous organization that will not only help you learn to be a good speaker; they also help you learn how to be a good leader. Personally, I think everyone should spend at least one year with Toastmasters – the skills you can learn are invaluable. Many of the well-known speakers in our community went through Toastmasters, people such as Wayne Dyer and Mike Dooley. Few people have natural speaking skills that can't be improved upon!

A newsletter

If you have information to offer people, a newsletter is a great way to get yourself known. You can either have some printed up at your local print shop or you can offer an internet newsletter. This only works if you have something to share that people are interested in. You also need to be a decent writer or people won't want to read what you have to say.

*"Whenever you find yourself hurrying, stop. Fix your attention on the mental image of the thing you want and begin to give thanks that you are getting it.
This exercise of gratitude will never fail
to strengthen your faith and renew your purpose."*
–Wallace D. Wattles, www.wallacewattles.wwwhubs.com/

Email Lists

This goes hand in hand with the newsletter. It is a good idea to start building an internet list. No one wants to get SPAM, so be sure whomever you put on your list wants to hear from you. Some people just add everyone to their list without asking. This is a good way to get ignored and to engender bad will instead of good will. Whenever you give a talk, pass around a sheet of paper where people can sign up to be on your email list. When you meet people or they ask for information about what you do, ask if you can put them on your list. If you do see internet addresses somewhere, email the people and ask if they would like to receive email from you.

It is a law that businesses must have some way to let people know they can opt out of future emails. I just add an informal note saying to let me know if you don't want to receive future emails.

There are companies that offer the service of sending out emails for you. One such company is called Constant Contact (www.constantcontact.com) and a lot of people have started using it. They keep track of your email list, send the email out when you want them to and have templates you can use for your newsletters and other information. The current cost for a list of 500 names is around $15 a month.

Advertising

Here I am referring to paid advertising whether in magazines, newspapers, radio, television, sides of buses, menus, etc… Here is my bias: I believe in advertising. Some people think I believe in it because I have owned (and do own) a newspaper. What is true is there was a period of about eight years when I did not own a newspaper and, guess what? I advertised – and quite successfully, I might add. In one case a business was not doing well at all. I started a regular advertising campaign and within six months there was a huge increase in business.

For advertising to be successful, it needs to be targeted to your specific audience; it has to be consistent; and it has to be placed in the same place often enough to have an effect (usually a year).

Whatever form you are considering, contact the business and ask for their media kit. This will give you information about the demographics of their readers, costs, discounts, etc.… Many businesses now have this information on their website. Even if you don't intend to advertise right away, get this information because it will come in handy for decision-making and planning.

When you analyze a publication, the size of their distribution does not always indicate whether or not they are a good place for you to advertise. Some people make the mistake of thinking a large readership means an ad will do better and this is not true all of the time. What matters is who reads the publication as well as how many people. Remember your ideal client? It is actually better to advertise in a smaller publication that is read by your targeted audience than it is to run ads in a huge publication with lots of readers who could care less about you.

I have seen some people spend thousands of dollars advertising in the "mainstream media" because they want to reach this audience. Yet what they are offering is not of interest to the "mainstream." They spent a lot of money putting their ads in front of people who were not aware enough to notice the ads or to respond to them.

"You might want to start each day by repeating the phrase, 'I believe the world is plotting to do me good today. I can't wait to see what it is.' And then look for the opportunities and the miracles."
–Jack Canfield, www.jackcanfield.com

Word of mouth

This is important for any business. Word of mouth works when you are good at what you do and have built (or are building) a good reputation. Liberal use of your business cards with current clients as well as offering referral incentives can help here.

Remember: word of mouth also works in reverse. One unhappy customer can spread a lot of negativity about you. If you know someone is not happy with you or your service it is worth your time and effort to try to work it out with the person. At least they will be able to say you gave them their money back or offered some other way to let them know you were sorry they were not happy. We all know there are some people who will complain no matter what. All you can do is give it your best effort at resolution, come from a place of integrity, and trust in the best outcome for all concerned.

Discounts and free stuff: could you? should you?

In today's world of Walmarts and the "big box stores," it is becoming increasingly difficult for the small business owner to "compete" on price. When a business is large with multiple locations, they can buy in quantity and pass along the savings to their customers. This is pretty hard to do when you are a small business with little or no room to navigate on your prices. And as our products and services continue to enter the mainstream marketplace "big" business gets into the act and is able to offer lower prices. Even small publications such as the one I own are running into situations where larger firms own five or more publications in different cities and can offer lower rates than we can. So, what to do?

First of all, don't even try to compete on price because you will not win. Focus on the quality of your service or product. Focus on attracting clients who will value you and your service/product and who are not just focused on price. (Remember when you made a list of the qualities of your customers/clients? Add this to the list as something you *want* in your customers and clients). If you start discounting your services in order to compete with the "big boys" you will eventually go out of business.

Having said that, it is wise to find ways to make introductory offers to new clients or to give your current clients a special "thank you." Maybe you could offer a discount for multiple visits (after nine massages they get the 10th one free or at half price, something like that).

How about having some give-aways for your clients that also serve as a marketing tool. Look at things such as pens, calendars, mugs, etc…. and see if there is something you could offer as an extra gift as opposed to cutting prices on your services.

What about clients who can't afford your services but want or need them? If you can, find a way to offer a sliding fee scale to a certain amount of clients on a monthly basis. If you can find a way to help such people without hurting your business, do it. The challenge here is to remember you are in business and if you give away the store you won't be there for other people – what good is that?

An important point to remember is that if people are buying based only on price then whoever they go to will lose that customer as soon as someone else offers a lower price or when the price is raised to its proper level.

Offer your product or service at a fair price. Be really good at what you do. If you can offer some incentives or gifts, do so. If you build your business on quality, you will build consistent customers who will respect you and remain loyal to you.

"Success is a state of mind. If you want success,
start thinking of yourself as a success."
–Dr. Joyce Brothers

What about trading and bartering?
Trading or bartering goods and services is very popular in our community. Sometimes it works and sometimes it doesn't. Here's my take on it.

If you can make an exact trade and IF you are trading for something you would have bought anyway, it can be a good situation for both parties. If your massage costs $60 and my massage costs $60 and if we were both going to get massages anyway, this trade works. If my massage costs $100 and yours costs $65 and if you already have a massage practitioner and don't want to get a massage from me, it doesn't work.

If you find yourself trading a lot you might discover yourself coming up short on cash when it is time to pay your bills. If everyone traded various services, trading on a large scale might work. But they don't. This is why money was invented in the first place. It is a neutral form of trading that everyone agreed to accept.

Using New Spirit Journal as an example, this is an issue we deal with a lot. People want to trade massage, Reiki, hypnotherapy, and other services for advertising in the newspaper. This doesn't work for us because our printer, the post office, landlord, and the phone company won't trade with us. They want money. If we traded advertising for services, we would quickly be out of business.

When you are considering making a trade with someone, carefully consider it before saying "yes" or you could find yourself with a lot of services or goods you aren't using and not enough cash to pay your bills!

Testimonials

Having current clients or customers give you a testimonial about your product or service is fabulous. People who are thinking about your service put weight in the fact that someone else thinks well of you or your product. When you use testimonials, it is best when you can use the person's full name, city and state. If the person does not want to have their name used, initials, with city and state are the next best thing. Be sure you have the person's name and their permission in case you ever need to produce it. It goes without saying that you should never make up testimonials.

"People rarely succeed unless they have fun in what they are doing."
–Dale Carnegie, www.dalecarnegie.com

"Success is not the key to happiness. Happiness is the key to success. If you love what you are doing, you will be successful."
–Herman Cain, www.hremancain.com

What about your "competition?"

It is a good idea to know what other professionals in your area of expertise are doing and charging for their services/products. Conventional wisdom would have you spending a lot of time on this step. I don't and here's why. Energy follows thought. When you spend a lot of time focused on your "competition," you are giving them your energy. I don't believe in competition at the big picture level. If you and your competition are providing the services you are here to provide, you are not in competition at all. People are attracted to different businesses for different reasons. Be yourself. Be good at what you do and attract your customers. Let your competition do the same!

Writing Your Marketing Plan

Now you are ready to write your marketing plan. Don't panic. This is not difficult. Larger companies use fairly complicated marketing plans and are involved in all sorts of market research. You don't need to do anything quite that complicated. The work you have already done in this course will make this next step easy and fun! Get your description of your ideal client in front of you. Have the list of possible marketing tools handy as well.

First of all, how much money can you spend on marketing every month for the next year? Whether it is $10 or $1,000, you need to know how much you can commit to marketing every month before you can begin to decide what you will do.

Once you know this figure, look at your list of possible tools and what these might cost you. What can you do? Business cards? A website? An ad in a publication or several publications? You might need to spend some time doing research first so you know how much different things cost.

Write down the things you can do to market your business, how often you will do them, and what it is going to cost you. Spend some time on this step. Look at how much time and/or money each thing will cost you and honestly assess if this is something you can commit to doing on a regular basis. Remember, you want to be able to do whatever it is for a full year.

Your plan might include the following:

- Have business cards made.
- Get my website operational and updated monthly.
- Join my local Chamber of Commerce and go to the meetings every month. Serve on a committee.
- Speak at my local Kiwanis, Rotary, and Lion's clubs – once each this year.
- Run an ad in _____ publication every month.
- Speak at _____ Bookstore or offer classes there.
- Hold an information meeting at my local library once a quarter. Advertise this by using flyers I place around the neighborhood.
- Offer to write a six-week series for my local newspaper.
- Conduct a survey of my current clients to see how they found out about me.
- Offer an incentive to my current clients for every new client they refer to me.
- Start a group of local _____ (Astrologers, massage practitioners, writers) so we can get together to support one another, make referrals, and share ideas.

After you have written down your plan, let it stew for a few days. Look at it, add, subtract, get it to the point that you feel it will work for you. There are many other ideas that I have not listed. Your particular area of expertise might lend itself to things I haven't even thought of. Whatever you think will work for you, give it a try.

"I don't know the key to success,
but the key to failure is to try to please everyone." –Bill Cosby

"Women will never be as successful as men because they have no wives to advise them." –Dick Van Dyke

Marketing is more of an art than a science. Yes, you can work the numbers but the truth is that following your instincts will generally take you in the right direction.

Creating a Market

Do you remember pet rocks (or hearing about them?). Who on earth even knew they needed or wanted a pet rock? Walk through any store and you will find products that were created because someone thought they could market the item to others. This is as opposed to products that are created in response to a true need – products such as food, clothing, and shelter.

If you have a product that has not been created in response to a current need then you will have to create a market for that product or service. This can also be the case if you bring your services to a new geographical area where it did not exist before.

"Your business is never really good or bad 'out there.' Your business is either good or bad right between your own two ears."
–Zig Ziglar

When you create a market rather than respond to a need, your job is different because then you have to show people that they want what you have to offer even though they may not have heard of it before. You will have to use more glitter and excitement to get people's interest. The actual techniques you use will be the same, but you will have to appeal to people's sense of adventure rather than to their sense of need.

To create a market, write down all the reasons someone might possibly want what you have. What unacknowledged need will your product meet? Or desire? What will it bring to people's lives that will give them joy, laughter, peace, financial abundance, or health? Once you can clearly state this, creating your marketing plan is the same as above.

Get Other People's Opinions

Find a few trusted friends and colleagues who will give you their honest opinions. These are the people you share your marketing ideas with before you launch them. Show them your business card, your website, your brochures….tell them you want their honest feedback. This does not mean you will necessarily make changes. Their input will help you clarify what you are doing and it will help you get some idea of how other people might respond to your materials.

Tips About Your Website

This information was prepared by Rhonda Dicksion at Indigo Dog Design and is fully copyrighted by her. Her website is www.indigodog.com. She did my website as well as many others you can see at her website.

Thinking about your own website?

While you are looking at options and putting together your thoughts and preferences, here are a few things for you to know and keep in mind:

• Websites are now a very important part of having a business. If you are like me, you often go to the web to get more information about a business. (Heck, you'll probably do that before you decide to hire me, right?) Your website is often the first impression you will make on a customer or client, so your site should be as representative of you as you can make it. Websites are an indispensable tool of business, and one of the best ways to promote your business or service.

• A good website can take the place of an institutional flyer or brochure. Websites can be changed very quickly and at much less cost than can printed materials. I very much recommend that you have a business card to hand out to introduce yourself and point people to your website, but if your budget doesn't allow for both brochures and a website, a website is the more practical and economical choice in the long run.

• Decide on a domain name that works for you. Your name should be easy to remember, as short as possible, and should relate to you or your business. The old rule of thumb is that businesses should be dot-coms, organizations are dot-orgs, and internet entities are dot-nets. There are now a lot of other
choices such as dot-cc, dot-us, and dot-tv, but I encourage my clients to find a dot-com name. These are the easiest for the public to remember and give you a higher level of prestige.

• You can check the availability of the name you choose by going to the main page at www. Networksolutions.com and typing in your name choice. If your choice of names is x'd out it has been taken; if there is a blank check box it is available. Don't register your site just yet; just check its availability.

• After you decide on a domain name, the name must be registered and web hosting paid for. Your website will cost $100 to register and host for a year. This is a yearly fee which is paid to a hosting company to keep your site online and is separate from web design costs.

• Who will do your website? You can do your website yourself
or you can hire a web designer to do the work for you. If you choose to do your own website you will need to learn html and/or purchase a web authoring program as well as photo editing software. The choice is similar to deciding between doing your own electrical work or hiring an electrician. In the long run, it is often much less expensive — and certainly less time consuming and frustrating — to hire a professional.

• Whom should I hire? Of course, I recommend that you hire me (grin), but any designer should be able to provide samples of their sites as well as referrals to clients. After conferring with you to discover your objectives with your website, a designer should give you an estimate as well as a reasonable time frame in which your site will be completed.

• Remember that the least expensive bid may not be the best way to go. Generally you pay for design work by the hour, and knowledgeable designers generally work much faster. Good design work is not inexpensive, but it will really pay dividends in the business it attracts. In addition, it's always best to hire someone with whom it is easy to communicate and who shares your vision.

• Determine your budget. If your web designer has some idea of your budget going into the project, she or he can work within that. A general rule of thumb is that you will probably pay as much for a website as you would for a television. The more features you want, generally the more expensive it will be.

• Do you have any websites you particularly like? Knowing what you definitely like and dislike will give your web designer ideas as to which way they should or should not go with your website design. Do you have favorite colors or want a particular feel for your site? Do you need multiple pages or want to be an affiliate? Let your designer know before you start.

• Be sure to communicate with your designer and let her know if she is on track. It's a lot easier to make changes or course corrections while the site is being built.

• Have fun with the process. From your website's inception to the time of completion, the entire process should have you doing dog-circles. Relax in and enjoy as your new creation unfolds!

End of This Week

What a busy week this has been. I hope you took advantage of this time to design your marketing plan. If you did, you now stand way above most people who market by the "seat of their pants" method. Next week, I will bring all of this together with a wide assortment of tips and ideas…and for the first time we will talk about money! Until then….

Week Five

There is so much that can be said about business, so many different areas to cover. My goodness, entire college degrees are given in the area of business! This last week I am going to cover many different topics that are important to your entrepreneurship! At the end I am adding a resource list that will give books and internet sites that I have found helpful over the years.

Use All of Your Tools

I am constantly amazed at how many people who are involved in holistically-oriented businesses don't use the tools they have, tools that will help them succeed in their business. I will mention a few here, ones I am sure you already know about. Are you using them?

"It isn't what you know that counts. It's what you do with what you know that matters!"
–Dr. Robert Anthony, www.drrobertanthony.com

Meditation: it doesn't matter what form of meditation you use. Spend time every day in the meditative state. Going into this space is the way to connect with your inner self and inner knowing. Make some form of meditation a staple of every day. From this practice will come the foundation you need to succeed.

Visualization: spend five minutes a day visualizing your success as if it was already yours. You don't need to spend hours at this for it to work for you. This is one of the oldest techniques in existence and it works. Ask any successful sports figure!

Affirmations: many people who have been on the spiritual path for awhile don't use affirmations because they think these are for "beginners." As long as you find your mind capable of getting onto a negative track you need affirmations! Affirmations help align your mind with your heart and spirit.

Journaling: keeping a journal is a fabulous companion along the road to success. Your journal doesn't need to be fancy. Every day write in it. Write down how you feel, and what you are thinking. It is a place to try out new ideas and new behaviors. I pull a tarot card every day and record it. Some people use angel cards or the I Ching or the Runes. After you have journaled for six months, go back and read your early entries. It is fascinating to see how much (or little) you have grown; to see if the same issues are bothering you or if you have moved on to new ones. I have my journals for the past 24 years in a trunk. I haven't gone through all of them in awhile but I do go through recent ones from time to time and find them an awesome source of insight into myself and my journey.

Success Journal: Have a special journal just for recording your successes, no matter how small or large they are. Pull it out when you are doubting yourself and your abilities. It is too easy to focus on what is wrong with ourselves. Keeping a success journal is a way to focus on what is right with you. And you know: "What you focus on expands!"

"The achievement of anything that you desire must be considered success, whether it is a trophy, money, relationships, or things. But if you will let your standard of success be your achievement of joy, everything else will fall easily into place." –Abraham
www.abraham-hicks.com

Celebrate your successes: When something good happens to you or your business, celebrate!!! Have a special lunch or dinner. Go to the movies. Buy special hot or cold drinks for your staff. Send thank you cards. Post signs in your business. Don't ignore even the smallest success. By celebrating and honoring your successes you open the floodgates for more!

List-making: many teachers talk about making lists of what you want or of your goals. There are many different ways to do this. Find one you like and use this tool. It is a wonderful way to keep yourself on track and to be able to cross off things and events as you manifest them.

Treasure mapping: making a collage or treasure map of what you want your life to be like is a great way to help your subconscious focus on what you want to attract into your life. If you don't want to make a large one for your wall, use a photo album and put pictures of what you want in the album.

Videos, CDs, internet courses, books: There is a large amount of information available to help you succeed. Vow to never stop learning. You can always expand your horizons. If you ever become the type of person who "knows it all," I feel sorry for you. Because you bought this course, I think you are the sort of person who will always be curious and open to new learning. Sometimes you learn about something you already know but you learn it in a new way – this is just as valuable as learning it in the first place.

"Believe that you will succeed. Believe it firmly and you will then do what is necessary to bring success about." –Dale Carnegie, www.dalecarnegie.com

Massage and bodywork: Budget to receive a massage or other form of bodywork at least once a month, more if you can. Operating your own business can be highly stressful. Using bodywork to help relieve the stress will support you to continue moving forward.

Aromatherapy, feng shui, colors, etc: There are many different techniques that can support you in your business. Find the ones that resonate for you and then use them!

Blessings and angels: Catherine Ponder is one of the most popular teachers who speaks about the power of blessing. Bless everyone you meet, bless your business daily, bless your money, your bank account, your customers, your "competitors." Become a blessing to everyone and watch your life blossom. You can't curse and bless at the same time. You can't bless and be thinking negative thoughts. When you place an ad, surround it with white light, bless it, and ask the angels to draw attention to it. When you post fliers, send emails, or use any other marketing techniques, send light, angels, and blessings with them. You will see results.

Form a Mastermind group: this idea was made famous by Napoleon Hill in his book "Think and Grow Rich." Basically, you find five or six people who are willing to support one another and you get together periodically to discuss your businesses.

Different groups have various rules and you can set it up however you want. The idea, though, is that this is a success group so you do not want to use it for therapy-type talking or as a place for people to unburden themselves of their negativity. It is a supportive thinktank. You can also start a Mastermind group that runs in your own mind - Napoleon Hill talks about this in his book as well. He had some famous people who were part of his mastermind group and he went to them for ideas and support!

"Be the success you want to become; live with the joy you want to achieve. Don't wait a moment longer to embrace the attitude that your life is a blissful adventure – even now." –Sandra Anne Taylor, www.sandraannetaylor.com

Vacations: take them! Be sure you give yourself time off from your business or it can drown you. Give yourself three-day weekends when you can. Observe the holidays. And be sure to go away several times a year. When you refresh yourself this way you will bring more to your business then if you let yourself get burned-out and too tired to think clearly. I know that in the early years of a business this sounds impossible. Find a way to take the time off anyway. It will serve you in ways I can't begin to explain!

Self-care: find ways to nurture yourself. Eat well, sleep enough, play, have hobbies, surround yourself with good friends, treat yourself to things that make you feel good. Too often entrepreneurs let the business become a monster that takes over their lives and end up being too tired or sick to enjoy their own success. Balance in all things. Work hard. Play hard. Life is to be enjoyed and success is a journey, not a destination. Have fun along the way!

Minding Your Manners

In our personal lives, most of us are aware of our manners – or at least we try to be. We say "please" when we want something and "thank you" when we get it. (Having said that, I also have to mention that I think basic manners are on the decline in our society-at-large and I would love to see them make a come back!) How does this apply to business?

Your customers and clients are people, just like you. They like to be treated with respect and they want to be acknowledged. Simple things like returning telephone calls and emails within 24 hours can go a long way towards making people feel they are important to you. If you won't be available for a few days, put a notice on your voice mail about when you will call back or have someone checking and returning calls for you. Put a notice on your email about when you will be back.

When someone does something for you, say thank you. When you want something from someone, add a please to your request. If you have to change an appointment, give at least 24 hours notice and be appreciative when the client (or provider) accommodates you. Respond to inquiries promptly. Many times it is the first person who responds who gets the business.

"You'll never get the approval you seek. You simply can't please everyone, so learn to please yourself and enjoy who you are." –Dr. Robert Anthony

If you have a retail business and have staff working for you, train them how to smile warmly at your customers. Teach them to be friendly. Help them understand that the customer is not the enemy: the customer pays their salaries! Teach them how to go the extra mile helping the customer find what they are looking for – even if your store doesn't carry it, help them find a place that does. Believe me, you won't lose a customer. They will remember who helped them and will come back to you!

Spend a little bit of time reflecting on ways you can mind your manners in your business. If you find areas that need some polishing, get out the cloth and go for it!

Small Goals-Small Steps

"Did she mean to write that? Aren't we supposed to have big goals and take big steps?" Sure, in the big picture of your vision you have big goals and it takes some big steps to reach those goals. But, what about on the everyday level? It is too easy to always be doing the big things (or trying to do the big things) and to forget that big projects consist of many smaller steps. Once we focus on the smaller steps it is much easier to reach our goals.

For instance, if you want to learn astrology or herbology or tarot, it can seem to be a huge task. But if you break it down into small steps, e.g., this week I will learn about lavender, before too long you will see that you have learned a lot! So it is with our businesses. If we can break our goals down into smaller steps and focus on those one at a time, we will not feel overwhelmed. And before you can say "The Entrepreneur's Toolbox," you will have reached your destination – or at least be a great deal closer!

Money! Money! Money!

What sort of course on business waits until near the end to talk about money? Isn't this what business is all about: money, and making lots of it? Yes and no – that is why this is at the end of the course. I didn't want you to be focused on money. Why? Because making money is the end result of having a successful business. It is true that some people go into business only for the purpose of making money. For most people who take this course, however, money is a byproduct of sharing their gifts with the rest of us. You have a sense of mission and purpose that is every bit as important as money.

Money is important and I enjoy it as much as anyone. The reason money is important, though, is because of what we can do with money – not the money itself. Imagine being stranded on a desert island alone with two million dollars in cash. How could this money help you find your way off the island? It couldn't unless you burned it to keep warm (wouldn't last very long) or unless a boat or ship showed up and you could pay them to take you away. In and of itself, the two million dollars is meaningless. Although this is more difficult to accept in the everyday world, it is still true. Money is only a means of exchange. Having a lot of it means you can exchange for more things and more experiences. But many times you can get those things and experiences without having money!

> *"You need not predict exactly how things will work out.*
> *All you need to do is desire, intend, and know it's possible,*
> *and it will be arranged to come to you."* –David Cameron Gikandi
> *www.imagesofone.com*

If you focus on your business, on serving people, on sharing the gifts you came here to share, the money will show up. I know this is difficult to hear when bills are due and you don't seem to have enough money to pay them, but it is true. This has been one of my major lessons this lifetime – truly understanding that money is a medium of exchange and nothing more! I have many stories I can tell you about how I was taught this lesson. I will tell you one of them here. See if you can remember something like this happening for you.

It was in the early days of my newspaper called The New Times. I had started the paper with no money and I had moved to Seattle where I knew two people. The first few years were total lessons in faith and trust. One of the most expensive parts of operating a newspaper is paying the printer. When I started the paper I was able to get credit from a printer because I had worked for them briefly in the past and they trusted me. However, at first they had told me they would give me credit for the entire amount for 30 days. The day before I was to print the first issue, they wanted half down. I was able to get a new friend to loan me the other half.

After a few months, though, my printing bill had grown. I was only able to pay about half or less every month. Finally, I was told that unless I brought $1,000 with me the next time the paper was to be printed, they would not print it. I had 30 days to come up with $1,000. I had no idea how I could do this. I asked people I barely knew if they would lend me the money and could not find it. The night before I was to go to the printer I was so sad. I didn't have the money. I had worked all month long "as if" I would have the money because I honestly thought I would have it.

I cried that night because I had worked very hard to make the paper the success it was becoming, people were starting to depend on the newspaper and the information it provided. I honestly couldn't believe that I would have been allowed to go as far as I had only to have to close the business down now. I went to bed wondering where my miracle would come from and doubting it would come at all.

I got up at 3:00 a.m. the next morning to drive to the printers. When I showed up I said hello to the people in the typesetting department. I noticed that the person who had given me the ultimatum wasn't there yet. I asked where he was. "Oh, he's out today, playing golf," I was told. "Is he coming in at all?" I asked. "No, he isn't."

I was stunned and stood there for a moment. No one was asking for the $1,000 dollars. "Ok," I said, "I guess we will get a move on and get this baby printed." And off I headed to the pressroom where the paper was printed. Within a few hours, the back of my car was full of 10,000 copies of the newspaper. I had gotten my miracle after all! I didn't need money to get that issue printed. By acting "as if" all month long and by believing I would be provided for, I was. This is, of course, a huge manifestation technique I learned first hand!

Of course, I still had to pay the printing bill and I did need the money to do that. How that happened is another story for another day. What's important is to realize I did not have to have the money when I thought I did in order to keep my business going.

"This is the secret to having everything. This is the essence of the power of acquiring wealth. Want it. Visualize it. Detach from it. Accept it. Open your heart and let the energy of the Universe flow through you. Become a hallow reed, and feel the power of Creation flowing through you."
–Tom and Penelope Pauley, www.richdreams.com

There are many courses available to help you with your money issues, whatever they might be. I mention several in the resources section of this course. If you can realize, though, that money is energy just like everything else is energy and focus on giving your gifts, the money will be there for you when you need it, sometimes in the most miraculous of ways!

Delegate

This is a major success secret. You are the genius behind your business. You are the person with the vision. Your talents are best used with the big-picture, not with the nitty-gritty things. Most entrepreneurs are hands-on people. We actually work in our businesses. Some of us are the only people in our businesses so how can we delegate? Once you are open to the idea of delegating tasks, the ways will show up for you. The first thing to do is make a list of all the things you don't particularly like doing in your business, things you would love to have someone else do. Did you know that there are people who love to do those things? And that at least one of those people is looking for you?

"The harder I work, the luckier I am." –Gary Player, www.garyplayer.com

I'll bet the money monster is rearing its ugly head about now. "How can I afford to delegate work when I can't even pay myself yet?" Oh, but when you are ready to delegate, when you are really willing to turn some things over to others, the way will be shown to you. Either the money will show up or a volunteer will show up or someone will want to do this for you in trade for something of value you have.

Until this happens, here's how to handle the things you don't enjoy doing.

Do them first! Reward yourself when they are done!

Whether is it dusting the store shelves, doing the bookkeeping, or writing ad copy: whatever it is you dislike doing put it at the top of your to-do list, get it done, then reward yourself with something special! Have a special tea or cookie that you get only when you complete one of these tasks. Have a special incense you burn only at those times. The reward doesn't have to be big and it doesn't have to be expensive: it just needs to be special and something you really, really enjoy. Before long, you will find yourself able to do the unpleasant tasks sooner, quicker, and with less grumbling. As soon as you can, find a way to delegate them!

Breaking Through Your Resistances

"Who me? Have resistances? No way. I want my success and I want it now!" I can hear you saying that loud and clear. If you are on this planet and if you haven't already done a lot of work on yourself, you have resistances to your own success. Resistance is part of the earth-game, part of what makes it so much fun and so maddening at the same time! And it shows up in the strangest of ways. For instance, the first day this course was available on the internet, it didn't work properly. I sent out an email telling everyone the course was available and what web page to go to only to receive emails back telling me people couldn't open the site. Groan. I got in touch with my webmaster and it was a simple fix, but in the meantime I was very embarrassed. Right away, I started asking myself how was I resistant to this course being a success and worked at releasing whatever blocks I had.

"If you are fully present, even in the face of a whirlwind, grace manages appropriately and effortlessly to take care of all aspects of manifestation."
–Brandon Bays, www.thejourney.com

There are actually several ways to look at resistance. One is to break through it and the other is to release it. Different people like to do this in different ways. There is a method called The Release Technique (www.releasetechnique.com) which is simply learning how to let go of whatever you are feeling, finding your true beingness, and living from that state constantly. Mike Dooley, who was in the movie The Secret, talks about blasting through blockages and resistances by just moving ahead and acting "as if." (www.tut.com) Both methods work. Which you use just depends on the situation and your temperament.

Sometimes people need therapy or counseling. If you have some deep-seated childhood issues, you might be well-served by getting into some sort of therapy with a qualified therapist. Choose one who believes in short-term work, though. If you are willing and if you are seeing a qualified therapist, there is generally no reason to see the person for five to ten years!

Remember: every time you start something new you are subject to your inner child, subconscious, or some other aspect of yourself kicking up a fuss and throwing roadblocks in your way. If you know this, it is much easier to handle the blocks with good humor and ease rather than letting them set you back or cause you to give up on your dreams.

Change course if you need to, amend your plans, whatever you feel you need to do, but do not give up unless and until you have hit such a wall that it is clear you are heading down the wrong road. And even then, be sure there aren't some side streets you are missing!

You're Succeeding: Now What?

You've done your work and the business is actually taking off and doing well. What's next? This can be one of the trickiest times for you. Once things start to work, it is easy to lean back in your chair and think that you will just enjoy your success. Yes, enjoy your success but remember that if you are not moving forward, you are moving backwards. You can't stand still.

> *"Abundance can be had simply by consciously receiving what already has been given."* –Sufi saying

As soon as you start to see some success, begin to plan for the next stage of the business. Do you want to open a second location? Add staff? Increase your line of products? Sell? Franchise? Start planning for the next step before you need to take it. Why? Because you want to keep your energy moving in a positive direction. If you are not planning for the next step, it won't be long before you find yourself bored and then it won't be long before you are in trouble. Once you are bored with your business, it is very difficult to keep it at a good level. Keep things exciting for yourself and plan the next stage before you get there!

It Looks Like You're Failing – Now What?

The first thing to do when things are not working is to STOP! Stop whatever you are doing and get away from the business. Take a day, a week, or even an afternoon: but, get away from the business. Go for a trip, a walk, or read a book or go to the movies. Even if you have to close the "shop" for a few days, let voice mail handle the calls, and stay away from email, it is worth it to give yourself some distance.

When things are not working in your business, the natural tendency is to sit down and start fretting about it, trying to figure out what you are doing wrong. There might not be anything wrong with your business. You could be in a natural slump. All businesses have cycles and thank goodness they do. No one can be in "Go" mode all the time. Just as we have seasons of the year, our businesses have seasons. It is not always harvest time.

By putting some distance between you and your business you give yourself and your business room for clarity to appear. Once you have given yourself a break, stay open to your intuition. Ask your business what is going on. From your place of calmness and clarity, let yourself look at the business and see what is happening.

> *"Add up all the moments you have no need. You will see that the moments in which you are free of need far outweigh the others."*
> –Lenedra J. Carroll, www.newworldlibrary.com

Are you in a natural slump? Is it time to revisit your marketing plan? Has something changed with your customer base in terms of what they want? How long has this been going on? What have you already done to change things? Are you getting tired of this business?

Spend some time really looking at your business. Then take action. If you are in a natural slump, use the time for planning and restructuring. If your client base has changed, research that and see how you want to respond to it. If you are bored, why? Do you need to change how you are operating, what you are doing? Take an honest look at your business and then adjust however seems appropriate.

What If Your Business Really Is Failing?

Sometimes a business is not going to work, no matter what you do, how clever you are, or how much it seems like it *should* work. Sometimes we are led to start a business for the experience itself rather than because the business is going to succeed! There is great wisdom in knowing when to get out of a business – or some aspect of a business – and move on.

I don't believe in failure, only a change of plans! Having said that, though, I will admit that when a business is not working and you have to shut it down it sure feels like failure! I have had a lot of successes in my life. Fortunately, I have had more success than failures, but I have had my share of businesses that did not work out. In each case, I was able to recognize what was happening and had the courage to move on.

It is embarrassing when a business doesn't work out. You feel like everyone is looking at you and saying, "What a loser she is! What made her think that would ever work?" Truth is, most people feel bad for you. Everyone knows how bad it feels when something doesn't work out. Don't let other people's opinions of you cloud your judgment. Sometimes the answer is to shut your doors and move on.

If nothing you try is working, if you have taken some time and really evaluated what is going on, if your "gut" says "enough!" it is time to move on.

"Sometimes the only way the Universe can move me from point A to point B is to move me through uncharted territory in time and space."
–Mike Dooley, www.tut.com

Once you shut the business down and have some time, sit down and write down what you learned from the change in plans. Whatever amount of money you lost, consider it the cost of your own private workshop! Sometimes these workshops are pretty expensive. One of mine was a second mortgage on a home to the tune of $40,000 – and that was in 1983 so in today's dollars it is a lot more. But what a workshop it was. I learned so much about business from that experience, things that I have been able to apply to successful enterprises I started after that.

Take the time to write down what you have learned while it is still fresh in your mind. As time passes, memories fade and you don't want to forget the precious lessons you learned. You paid enough for them in terms of dollars and sweat so be sure you get the value from the experience.

If you feel embarrassed, here is something to think about. I am sure you have heard of Nightingale Conant Corporation. They are one of the biggest purveyors of self-help and business programs that exist. A few years ago they started a publication called AvantGarde. People could subscribe to it online and/or to the print edition. I like to hold what I am reading so I got the print edition as well as the online one. After about six months, I got a letter in the mail telling me they had decided to stop publishing the print version because it no longer suited their plans. They were mailing me a $10 voucher I could use at their website. There was no further explanation. Obviously, they had not been able to attract the advertisers they needed to support the print version.

"Infinite Spirit, open the way for my immediate supply, let all that is mine by Divine right now reach me, in great avalanches of abundance. Give me a definite lead, let me know if there is anything for me to do."
–Florence Scovel Shinn

There was no wailing or gnashing of teeth. Well, maybe there was at the home office but not in front of us, the customer. They simply made a business decision and acted on it. As a customer I was sorry because I enjoyed the print version, but I accepted their decision and didn't think any the less of them for it.

If you have to close your business down, just do it, take the lessons, and move on. It is not the end of the world. There will be other opportunities, probably better ones!

Getting a Job

After you shut down a business you might have to get a job again. If you are an entrepreneur you will have a business again. Being an entrepreneur is in a person's blood and a silly thing like failing won't keep you from starting another business. If because of things like mortgages, car payments, and food you need to get a job, go ahead and get one. You might want to downplay the fact that you just owned a business. Many businesses don't like to hire entrepreneurs because they know you will leave and start another company! On the other hand, there are positions where the spirit and knowledge of an entrepreneur is exactly what the company is seeking. Do your homework before you apply for any job.

While you are employed by someone else, learn everything you possibly can that you might be able to use in your next venture! One time I didn't own a business for eight years. I was so frustrated because I had sold a successful business and started another one, only to have that one be a disappointment. I went back to work for someone else, something I never thought I would have to do. The Universe had great things in store for me, though. I learned so much in those eight years, things I could not have learned any other way, things that help me even today, things that you see in this course! I even learned how to think in terms of millions of dollars when I managed a multi-million dollar operation! That experience taught me to think bigger than I had in the past.

Selling Your Business

When most people start a business they don't think they will sell it. They aren't even thinking in that direction. It is a good idea to think about selling your business long before the sale happens, if indeed it does. Why? Because thinking this way takes your thinking to a higher level which will help you succeed in larger ways. It also gets your personality out of the way a little bit and helps you be more detached from the day-to-day details of the business. It helps you think more like a true business person rather than a employee.

If you are seriously thinking about selling your business, I want you to do something before you make one move in the direction of selling. I want you to take a month's vacation. More often than not you don't really want to sell your business. You are probably burned out. You probably need to expand your business and your horizons.

Let me tell you a story. I started a business with no capital, in a new city where I didn't know anyone. It was very difficult and I learned a lot. And the business grew and succeeded. I lived, ate, and breathed my business. It was the fulfillment of my heart's desires. I couldn't imagine myself ever doing anything else.

"If at first you don't succeed, think how many people you've made happy."
–H. Duane Black

After ten years, I got itchy feet and felt it was time for something new. I didn't know what. I tried teaching classes and doing tarot readings. I was exhausted after ten years of being so involved in my business. Yes, I had taken a few vacations but never more than a week at a time and I never really got away from the business. I was commuting two hours a day, one-way, and had been doing that for eight years.

One day the idea came to me to sell my business and use the money from the sale to start another, unrelated business, closer to home. I took all the necessary steps, found a buyer, and sold the business. This took almost a year. During that time I wondered if I was doing the "right" thing and lots of incidents happened to slow down the process. But, I never stepped back long enough to clear my head.

Once the business was sold and I had been away from it a month or so, I was filled with regret and wondered what on earth I had done. This business had been my baby. I had poured my heart and soul into it. Now it was gone. It took years for me to forgive myself and to move beyond the feelings of regret I had.

Would things have gone differently if I had gotten away from the business long enough to get past the burnout? Would I have found a different way to handle my itchy feet? Sure, everything works out for the best and today I am at peace with what happened. But I think one of the reasons it did happen was so I could share it and write this for you!

If after getting away from your business for a month you still want to sell it, here are the steps to follow.

First of all, have your business appraised by a professional business appraiser. Any reputable buyer is going to want to pay a fair price just like you want to get a fair price. If you just pick a figure out of the air or decide on one you think is fair, the price could be too high which would scare off potential buyers, or it could be too low which would not be fair to you. It is well worth the price of an appraisal to know what you should get for your years of hard work and dedication. Google "business appraisers" to find someone geographically close to you or someone who specializes in your type of business.

"It takes 20 years to make an overnight success."
–Eddie Cantor

There are business brokers (use Google again) who work similarly to real estate agents. There are many advantages to using a broker (I didn't use one), but for most small businesses you will be able to find a buyer on your own. Navigating the actual sale of the business only requires the help of a lawyer to draw up the papers. Generally, the small business owner can handle this on his or her own. If your business has any complex aspects to it, though, you are probably better off to use a broker.

Selling your business is not much different from writing your marketing plan. Once you know your price range, sit down and write up the profile of the person who might want to buy your business and someone you would want to sell it to. If you have been personally involved in your business, you know the sort of person it will take to operate it successfully. Then research the ways to reach that person: advertising, emailing friends and business associates, etc....

Prior to meeting with people, write down the procedure you will follow. You will need to have a packet of information ready for the person. You will also ask them to sign a confidentiality agreement before giving it to them since it will include some financial data you might not want to share with others. When you speak to the person on the phone or through email, have a list of questions ready that you want to ask and be prepared for their initial questions. The asking price for the business will be one of them so be prepared to discuss price right off the bat. If the person indicates they can afford the business, ask them to bring some sort of proof or financial statement from their bank. Be very firm about this. You do not want to waste your time talking to someone who cannot afford to pay your price.

*"In order to succeed you must fail,
so that you know what not to do the next time." – Anthony D'Angelo*

After you have found the person you think you want to sell the business to, spend some time with them, get to know them. Find out if they have a spouse or partner who will be involved with the business. If so, get to know that person. You might spend a lot of time getting to know the potential buyer, feel good about the person, and then as soon as the sale is over find out they intend to have someone else involved, someone you might not have approved of. Remember: your business is only a heartbeat away from being in the hands of this person's spouse, child, or partner. Be comfortable with everyone involved or keep looking. You didn't spend years building your business only to have it fall into the hands of someone who doesn't respect what you have done and who might cause the subsequent demise of the business.

Whether you are buying or selling a business, get a copy of *Strategies for Successfully Buying or Selling a Business* by Russell L. Brown. The author is a successful business broker and this book is a goldmine of information that will help you navigate these waters successfully.

Franchising Your Business

Franchising might be the next step for your business. Although it can be a fairly complicated process, for some people it has opened unexpected doorways to success. In order to be able to franchise your business it not only has to be successful. You have to be able to package your business in such as way that someone else can set up one just like it somewhere else and, using your model and instructions, be successful too. Not all businesses lend themselves to the franchising model and some require very specific skill sets in order to succeed.

"Somehow I can't believe there are many heights that can't be scaled by a person who knows the secret of making dreams come true. This special secret can be summarized in four C's. They are: curiosity, confidence, courage, and constancy, and the greatest of these is confidence."
–Walt Disney

Although I have not owned or built a franchise, I did work for two different ones in which I was an employment consultant. In both cases, the people who set up the franchises provided cookie-cutter ways of doing business that worked. It still took hard work and smarts to succeed but the owners of the franchises had a success system that someone else had already built, one they could count on. They were also able to turn to the head office for help when they needed it.

If you are thinking of franchising your business or if you are thinking of buying one, here are two helpful books on the subject. *Franchising: Pathway to Wealth Creation* by Stephen Spinelli. *Franchising and Licensing: Two Powerful Ways to Grow Your Business in Any Economy* by Andrew J. Sherman.

Resources

Over the years I have read many books and listened to tons of audio programs. There is so much good information available it can be intimidating. I went through my various books and programs and I have chosen the ones I think have been most helpful to me and to my clients. I have avoided listing ones that require a lot of money or that require you to travel or be away from your business any length of time. Many of these are not business-specific but contain information vital to your success in business.

I am sure there are some excellent ones not mentioned here. If you have favorites you think I should include in future editions of this course, please feel free to send them to me.

Books (not listed in any particular order):

- Ask and It Is Given by Esther and Jerry Hicks
- The Law of Attraction by Esther and Jerry Hicks
- The Success Book and The Abundance Book by John Randolf Price
- Thinkertoys, A Handbook of Business Creativity by Michael Michalko
- The Power of Intention by Wayne Dyer
- Think and Grow Rich by Napoleon Hill
- Quantum Success by Sandra Anne Taylor
- The Success Principles by Jack Cornfield
- Spiritual Economics by Eric Butterworth
- The Prosperity Secrets of the Ages by Catherine Ponder
- Creating Money by Sanaya Roman and Duane Packer
- The Attractor Factor by Joe Viatle
- The Science of Getting Rich by Wallace Wattles
- The Master Key System by Charles J. Haanel
- Living by Grace by Joel Goldsmith
- Time Management by Julie Morgenstern
- Radical Forgiveness by Colin Tipping
- Radical Manifestation by Colin Tipping
- You Can Have It All by Arnold Patent
- One Minute Millionaire by Mark Victor Hansen and Robert G. Alllen
- The New Science of Getting What You Want by Doug D'Anna
- Wealth Consciousness by Roger Lamphear
- The Nature of Personal Reality by Jane Roberts
- I'm Rich Beyond My Wildest Dreams, I am! I am! I am! By Tom Pauley and Penelope Pauley
- Managing for Dummies
- Wealth Beyond Reason by Bob Doyle
- The Good Timing Guide, An Astrological Business Planner by Madeline Gerwick
- The Essential Drucker by Peter F. Drucker

CD/Tape Sets (not listed in any particular order):

- It's Never Crowded Along the Extra Mile by Wayne Dyer
- The Principles of Everyday Grace by Marianne Wiliamson
- Creating Miracles Everyday by Richard Carlson, Ph.D.
- The Ultimate Brain by Tom Kenyon (Experiential)
- Action Strategies for Personal Performance by Brain Tracy
- The Abundance Course by Larry Crane
- Infinite Possibilities by Mike Dooley
- Leveraging the Universe and Engaging the Magic by Mike Dooley
- Paraliminals (various) Learning Strategies Corporation

Internet Sites (not listed in any particular order):

www.tut.com
www.richdreams.com
www.releasetechnique.com
www.boundlessliving.com
www.simplemeditation.com
www.radicalforgiveness.com
www.nightingale.com
www.robertanthonyonline.com
www.learningstrategies.com
www.abraham-hicks.com
www.psycho-cybernetics.com
www.imagesofone.com
www.newspiritjournal.com

Other:

Your local Chamber of Commerce is a great source of information as well as of various workshops and people who can support you.

An organization called SCORE has retired business executives who will help you for free or for a nominal fee. They offer workshops on everything from how to set up your business to marketing and taxes. The national website is: www.score.org. From there you can locate the office closest to you.

We Are At the End of This Course

Has it really been five weeks since we started this journey together? Hard to believe, but that is true. Thank you for following your heart and living your dream of being in business for yourself. The planet is better for your being here. I know that being an entrepreneur is not the easiest path in the world and I know that few of us ever make it "big." But it is the small business owner such as yourself that contributes so much to the world. I hope this sharing of ideas and techniques that I have done is helpful to you. There is so much more I could tell you but I guess that will have to wait for another course and another time.

Above all else, have fun in your business. The day you stop having fun is the day you need to step away and reevaluate what you are doing and why. Life is meant to be good and it can be. Follow your heart. Use your head. And I will see you somewhere on the path.

The next page contains an evaluation of this course. Any feedback you give is greatly appreciated! Thanks in advance!

Blessings,
Krysta
krysta@krystagibson.com

The Entrepreneur's Toolbox

Course Evaluation

It would be very helpful to me and future readers if you could take a few minutes and answer the following questions. You can email them to me or print this out and mail them to me. You can remain anonymous. If you do want a response from me, let me know. Thanks in advance.

Krysta Gibson
krysta@krystagibson.com
14911 Chain Lake Rd #431
Monroe, WA 98272

1. Please tell me three things you liked about the course?

2. Please tell me three things you would change about the course?

3. Was it too long?

4. Was it too short?

5. Information you wish had been here but wasn't?

6. You would or would not recommend this course to others?

Krysta Gibson

Appendix

These are some articles I have written that address a variety of business-related topics. Over the years people have told me this information is helpful. As my thanks to you for purchasing The Entrepreneur's Toolbox, I am including them for you to read. All articles are by Krysta Gibson and fully copyrighted.

Letting there be peace in your business

If you've been in business for awhile or even had your practice more than two days, you know that having it be a peaceful experience isn't the easiest thing to do. This is particularly humorous for those of us involved in "alternative" areas of service. We purport to want to help bring peace and love to the planet but sometimes find it difficult to bring this to our own place of business or to our own families. Here are a few ways you can make your business a more peaceful and loving experience.

Live and work from big-picture consciousness rather than from a little one. Peace among all nations and individuals isn't going to happen in a day and you won't build a successful practice or thriving store in one day, either. When you get too close and lose your balance, float away to a star and look down at yourself, your life, and your business. This puts things back in perspective quickly.

Slow down. We create more stress and heartache for ourselves and others by rushing. I have found I actually accomplish more when I think and move in a slow and methodical manner than when I rush around in a panic – even while trying to meet deadlines. It helps to remember that we live in eternity. Time is not going to end and neither are we, so what's the hurry?

Apply some order to your life; make a schedule and follow it. Nothing disturbs peace as quickly as not knowing where you're going or how you intend to get there. Have a plan for your business and for your day. Follow it with creative flexibility. Some folks don't like to plan because they feel this robs them of serendipity. To the contrary, when we have a plan, energy is released so we can explore the back roads and side streets we find along our way. Because we have a plan, we can find our way back to the main highway whenever we want to do so!

If your finances are in a shambles, if you are deeply in debt and can't see your way free, take some action to correct the situation. Anyone drowns quickly in panic and despair. See a financial aid consultant, a prosperity teacher, or other type of counselor. Contact your creditors and make arrangements to pay them, even if only a small amount each month. Peace will return quickly even if it takes awhile to pay everyone and return to a positive cash flow. Simply knowing you are in the process of achieving financial stability will bring you peace of mind and heart.

Be kind to yourself and to your customers, clients, friends, and family. Aw, heck, be nice to strangers, too! Make harmlessness in thought, word, and action a priority in your life and watch peace make a beeline for your heart. I know how hard it is to think nice thoughts about people when they are being mean to you, but this is exactly what I am asking you to do. Peace begins in the mind of every person on this planet. If someone is projecting negativity towards you, the best response is to send that person love and acceptance. You may not see a positive result right away, but it will be there.

Remember you are a lightworker or you wouldn't be reading this. You are here for a very definite purpose which is most likely being met through your business. Relax into this, knowing that your higher self has the answers you need.

Meditate/pray daily. I am amazed at how many people in turmoil have approached me over the years and when I ask if they meditate every day they say they used to but don't any more because they are too busy. I say they feel too busy because they are not taking the time to find their center. It is important to take at least a few minutes at work and at home every day to turn within. That is where peace is waiting for you. If you don't know how to meditate, contact the Ananda Center in Seattle or take some other similar classes offered by churches and teachers in your area. If you don't live close to such a place, there are many tapes and CDs available such as Wayne Dyer's *Getting in the Gap*. Find what suits you and use it.

Not everyone is a writer, but finding a way to express how you feel and think is a great way to navigate the waters of life. Some people like to write three pages in longhand every day as discussed in *The Artist's Way* by Julia Cameron. By allowing themselves a free stream of consciousness, they are able to safely release thoughts and feelings that would otherwise cause upset during the day. I know one person who has an e-mail buddy. They send one another lengthy e-mails talking about their thoughts, feelings, and experiences. Although they have never met and live in different states, they have found a way to be sounding boards for one another and find this communication helps to ground and center them.

Finally, give open-heartedly of your time and talents without allowing yourself to be used or abused by others. Giving of ourselves to others in appropriate ways helps us to forget the smaller troublesome details of our business and lives and allows us to focus on what is truly important. Find a cause you can support with time or money. Some people like to support their local food bank or homeless shelter while others give to peace groups, churches, or other such organizations. Peace flourishes with generosity and so will your business.

Advertising is like going fishing!

When I was the publisher/owner of *The New Times* newspaper in Seattle, some people would place an ad and say, "I'm just going to run an ad once and see how it goes. If it works, I'll run it again." In some cases, the person had wonderful response to the first ad. Sometimes – often – their expectations were not met! This method of advertising is like playing Russian roulette with one's advertising dollars. Marketing research has shown that there are better ways to get the results you want. Advertising is like going fishing.

Imagine for a moment…a person decides to go fishing. What do they do? First, he or she decides on the type of fish they want to catch. This determines what lake, river, or ocean they will go to. It also determines whether they can fish from a pier, the bank or shore, or if they will need to take a boat. Bait is the next concern – what will interest the fish the person wants to catch? Once all of these issues have been dealt with, it is time to go fishing.

Let's say they have chosen to fish in a lake and took their boat with them. Can you imagine the person rowing to the middle of the lake, baiting their hook, throwing the line, waiting five or ten minutes, pulling the line in with no fish on it…and then saying, "Oh, nothing is biting here," then rowing to shore and going home? Not in a million years!

When the first cast didn't work, the fisher would try a few more. If they still didn't get even a nibble, they would evaluate the situation. Should they change bait? Should they use a lure? Did they wait long enough to give the fish a chance to notice the bait? Maybe the fish were just getting ready to bite. Are they in water that is deep enough? Should they move to a different part of the lake? Are the fish they want to catch even in this lake? Maybe someone else just left this area and the fish have full bellies and aren't hungry. An evaluation is done and a new course of action is taken.

It is similar with advertising and marketing efforts. When one type of ad or course of action doesn't work, instead of putting our gear away and going home, we try another approach.

One of the secrets of successful marketing, something which most people do not utilize, is the concept of testing. In order to find out what works for our businesses, we need to be willing to test: test headlines, copy content, ad sizes, special offers (if appropriate for your type of business), pricing, location, and audience. Don't test everything at the same time, though, or you won't know what it was that made the difference. Decide on a particular concept, ad, placement, offer, etc., then play with the headline.

Which one draws the most response from the sort of client/customers you are seeking? If it works, keep using it. If it doesn't, try something else. Over time, test different types of offers, new concepts, etc… Let the public tell you what works by their response. After all, they are the experts at knowing what attracts them to your business and what doesn't.

Happy fishing!

What to do when discouragement sets in

No matter who we are or what we're doing, everybody experiences discouragement sometimes. Things don't move along as quickly as we'd like them to. A cherished goal always seems just out of reach. We're constantly faced with dead-ends or detours. What can we do in these situations?

When, despite our best efforts, things just don't seem to want to go our way, we need to stop. Just stop everything. Quit trying, quit thinking, quit pushing. Get away from the situation. Close your business for a few days if you have to, but put some distance between you and what you're trying to accomplish.

Many times this one action will allow the solution to emerge. When we're too close to a challenge, it can be impossible for us to relax enough to allow a pathway to open before us. Taking some time away from what's going on releases some of the pressure, allowing our creative juices to begin flowing again. Give yourself some space and see if answers don't present themselves unbidden. After all, they're already there- you're just too stressed to see them!

Discouragement can be a signal that we're too invested in the outcome of what we're doing. It can mean we have too much of our earthly egos involved and need to practice some detachment. Sometimes we think we know what we "should" be doing when the truth is we're way off base. If you're feeling discouraged, try a good dose of detachment from the outcome of what you're doing. Declare to the Universe that you want to be doing the higher will. If that is what you are doing and part of doing that means some struggle and dissatisfaction, fine. Declare that if you have misunderstood Higher Will and need to be on a different path, you are ready to be shown that. Then continue with your work and watch for feedback from the Universe. In a short time, you will know which way to go.

Are you following your bliss or are you doing what is expected of you? Discouragement set in really badly when we're trying to do what others want instead of what our heart wants. Be honest with yourself. If you're in people-pleasing mode, get clear on your true path and start following it. Ultimately, everyone will be happier, especially you.

Discouragement can be a delightful gift, showing us new ways to grow and to learn. It can be a tool that encourages us to become more than we thought we could be. Welcome discouragement when it comes. Sit with it rather than trying to push it away. You might be surprised at the gift it holds for you.

Flowing with the go of your business

It is very much a part of our culture to try to be bigger and better, to grow as fast as we can, to do, to produce, to make a huge splash. It's easy to carry this attitude and brashness to the world of your spiritually-based business. Many people run their businesses this way and it seems to work for them. Others try it and find themselves losing their values, ethics, and sense of self.

I believe every business is an entity onto itself and we are stewards of our businesses. I define a business as any enterprise we engage in for which we receive payment of some kind. By this definition, counselors are in business and so are ministers! Every business has a deva or angel who is responsible for the overall purpose and functioning of the business. It is our responsibility to contact the soul or overriding energy of our business and discover what it wants to do, when it wants to do it, and how.

This mindset is in direct contradiction to most business practices which state we should tell the business what to do. It is also in direct contradiction to many metaphysical teachings which tell us to take control of everything in our lives and design them the way we want them to be. Flowing with our business means finding out what the business wants to do and then using all of our powers and abilities to accomplish that.

Some people get nervous about this because they think it means they might have to do some things they would rather not do. Although that is possible, it is unlikely. If we have been paired up with a particular business, it is because we have the talents and abilities for it. Generally, whatever it wants to do will pretty much work for us as well.

Sometimes a business wants to actively grow and branch out while at others it wants to rest and enjoy feeling its roots growing slowly, gaining a firmer stand wherever it is. If we are experiencing frustration with our business, it could be that we are out of sync with what it wants to do. We might be trying to push it when it really wants to take off in new directions.

It is important to get in touch with our business' deva or angel. If this is a new concept for you, or one you have forgotten, start setting aside ten to fifteen minutes a day strictly for communication with your business. Write down ideas you are given. Ask questions about any difficulties or challenges you are facing. Try "channeling" your business in writing and see what it says to you!

Here are some questions to get your started:
- What is your purpose? What are we trying to accomplish together?
- Do you want to grow right now or do you want to rest? If you want to grow, in what way? What do I need to do to facilitate this?
- Is there anything I should be doing differently right now?
- What changes, if any, do you want to make?
- If there are specific challenges being faced, ask what can be done about them.

- If a decision needs to be made, ask for input and ideas.
- For a particularly delightful session, have a "meeting" with your business, yourself, your personal guides and angels, and whatever Masters are working with you right now. This one takes a bit more time, but is great for developing your listening muscles and expanding your concepts of what is possible.

Remember to write down everything or talk into a tape recorder because this is the sort of information easily lost when your attention returns to the day-to-day details of life. When you try doing this for awhile, I think you'll discover that working this way is actually a lot of fun and very exciting. It is light-years beyond worrying, fretting, and trying to carry the load yourself. Although some of your initial answers might be colored by your ego, continued practice with the technique will help you break through to a purer level of information.

We're never alone with any aspect of our lives, but especially not with our businesses. We are in partnership with them. If you are doing anything of a spiritual nature, it is because you have a special role to play on the planet right now. Doesn't it make sense to use every possible form of help available? Instead of running your business and telling it what to do, try reversing the process. Flow with your business for a change, listen to it, and see what happens.

How to tell if advertising dollars are being well-spent

Many times a business advertises simply in order to have a presence. A tally is not kept of responses to the advertising. The owner or manager can tell by the general volume of business whether or not their ad is working sufficiently for them.

However, in some businesses it is easy to keep a record of advertising response and when we can, it is wise to do so. Then we can tell which ads are working in which media. We can also tell if a formerly successful ad quits working and we need to change our style.

But how do we judge our response? Is it as simple as the number of phone calls we get or the number of people who walk through the door? Not always.

Years ago when I first started *The New Times* newspaper, I had an experience which brought this home to me. A massage therapist complained that his ad hadn't worked. In a month he had only one client come to see him as a direct result of the ad. At the time the rate for a classified ad was $3.00 for 20 words or less. He had run a $3.00 classified ad. I asked him how much he charged for a massage. "Sixty dollars," he replied. "So," I said, "in one month you invested $3 and got a return of $60? I think there are a lot of investors who would be very jealous!"

When you are evaluating your results in terms of money, it is important for you to figure out how much each client is worth to you. For instance, in this fellow's case, if he charges $60 for a massage and his average client gets one massage a month, then his average customer will spend $720 a year. If the average client stays with him for an average of two years, the client is worth $1440! This helps determine how much money can be spent on generating one client. In this situation, an advertiser might reevaluate and decide he can afford to spend more to generate clients like this.

Another advertiser I know placed a display ad and spent $115.20. She quit running the ad because she got only one client. That one client has already spent $720 with her in a year and a half and referred another client who has spent $90 in the past six months. $115.20 gave a return of $820. What if she had continued to advertise and picked up one good customer a month?

To evaluate your advertising budget, figure out how much each client or customer is worth to you over a period of time. This tells you how much you can afford to invest in attracting them to you. Think long-term rather than only immediate benefit and you'll be able to evaluate your advertising results in truly realistic terms.

Marketing ideas that don't cost a lot of money

Marketing yourself and your business doesn't have to be an expensive proposition. The most important thing to remember is that everything you do or say regarding your business markets you in some way. Metaphysically, of course, we know that everything we think and feel imparts energies to our projects. I am not talking about that here, though. I am assuming that you are working with visualization, affirmations, clearing blockages, healing personal issues, and so on.

The following ideas are meant to be a few third-dimensional things you can do to market your business without spending a lot of money.

1. Business cards are a basic marketing tool. Be sure the cards you use reflect you and your values and that enough information is presented so people get a sense of what you do. Carry some with you wherever you go. Give them to people whenever possible and put them up on bulletin boards when you can. Proper and regular use of your business cards is still one of the cheapest ways to market yourself.

2. Flyers and/or brochures, which give a clear explanation of your business, are invaluable. Take the time to work with your material and be willing to rework it as your business changes and grows. Remember that your brochure **is** you in people's minds. It is worth giving your best effort. Hand or mail it out whenever you can and post it in as many places as possible. There are a lot of good bulletin boards around –even regular grocery stores can be a great place to post your flyer or brochure. I know of a person who regularly rides the bus and routinely leaves one of her flyers on the seat. Another person leaves a flyer with her tip in restaurants. Brainstorm and you can come up with all sorts of creative – and legal – ways to make your presence known in the world so people who need to find you can do so.

3. The telephone can be a great tool for some people. There are some services that can't be easily marketed over the telephone, but many can. People who offer services such as bodywork can call therapists and let them know what specialty areas are offered. Therapists can explain their services to professionals such as physicians and chiropractors. Think of people who might be able to give you referrals (and vice versa) and network with them on the telephone as well as in person.

4. Word of mouth carries tremendous power, so anything you can do to get folks talking about you and your business in a positive way is really low-cost marketing. How do you get people to say nice things about you and recommend you?
    a. Be really good at whatever it is you do. Be constantly perfecting your craft and people will be sure to recommend you to their friends and family.
    b. Be service-oriented. How much more can you do or offer to your customers and clients that will cause people to talk about you? Be

creative. Be outrageous. I knew a massage therapist who had a portable hot tub that her clients could sit in for ten or fifteen minutes before their massage – at no extra cost. She used floral sheets instead of plain white ones and she misted the room with the scent of flowers. You can believe she was talked about and recommended. Of course, she also gave great massages!

    c. Can you offer discounts? Not every business is able to do this and sometimes it can backfire on you because then people resent paying the regular price. If you can give some special pricing some of the time, it does encourage people to try your service and then you have a chance to win a new customer. A word of caution here: it is usually not a good idea to give a price break to new customers if you don't offer it (or something similar) to your regulars. Why? People who have been frequenting your business can feel irritated when new folks are given special consideration. Let your regulars know you appreciate them as much as you do new people.

    d. Is there anything you can give away? Free bookmarks? Pamphlets? Calendars? Pens? Notebooks? Can you hold monthly drawings or contests? Think of creative ways to generate excitement among your customers. When you can, make it fun to do business with you. I realize this doesn't apply as readily to therapists or health professionals as easily as it does to bookstores and others, but even these folks can think of appropriate ways to let their clients know they are appreciated.

5. Free publicity can sometimes be obtained through press releases. Many smaller publications don't use press releases due to limited space. However, mainstream dailies and weeklies have been known to use such press releases when they have available space. If you have something interesting going on, write up a brief press release and send it to the local newspapers, television, and radio stations. It is a good idea to go to the library and get a book on writing press releases since poorly written ones will more likely hurt your cause than help.

6. Unusual ideas, products, and services generate interest. If there is anything you can add to your basic business or if you can package it a bit differently, people will tend to notice you.

7. Advertise. I mention this last only because this is a service I offer and I didn't want to seem self-serving. However, remember the mainstream saying "…..work like hell and advertise." It is true. I have taken over several operations that were doing poorly and started a regular advertising campaign that did not cost a lot. Within six months, the businesses were back on the map and doing great! I offer advertising because I believe in it and I know it works as long as it is one part of your overall marketing campaign and not the only thing you do!

Marketing doesn't have to be an intimidating chore you'd rather not do. It can be a fun and exciting part of your business and helps you do your work in the highest manner possible. After all, what's the point of being here if the people you need to reach can't find you? Happy marketing!

Krysta Gibson

Minding your manners

If you want to build your business, if you want to be respected, if you want to treat people well, one of the most important things you can do is have good manners!

You'd be amazed at the people who have alienated clients and customers – not to mention friends and family – by not saying please and thank-you or by not returning phone calls in a timely way! We've all been taught these simple manners, but we get involved in our businesses and our daily dramas and our minds go blank.

When someone does something nice for you, say thank you or send them a thank you note. With all the e-mail being sent these days, you'd be amazed at how impactful a handwritten thank-you note sent via snail mail can be!

One time I heard from a woman who had sent out over a hundred letters, telling people about a free seminar she was giving, a seminar which could have helped people with their businesses. She asked for an RSVP. Not one person responded. She was shocked.

She was a potential client and referral source for every one of the people she contacted. Can you imagine how a person would have shone in her eyes had they simply picked up the phone to tell her they were not able to attend her free workshop?

Then there are the folks who go away on vacation. A new client calls and leaves a message on their voice mail, voice mail which says nothing about the call not being returned for a week or more.

Can you imagine how hard it is for some people to get up the courage to call you in the first place? Then they sit and wait for your return call, not knowing it won't come. How easy it would be to leave a message saying calls won't be returned for a week. Better yet, what about having someone return calls for you in your absence? You don't have to say you are out of town and invite thieves to come in and have a party in your home or business. Simply say when the call will be returned. People don't do this and then they are upset when they call the person back and she is working with another therapist or has gone to a different business. Why shouldn't they? You didn't call them back.

I think one of the reasons people have such poor manners is because they are not having enough fun. Their own needs for delight are not being met so how can they meet those needs in others! Here are some ways to have more fun with your business. Lighten up and it will be easier to treat people the way you want to be treated.

1. Choose your favorite spiritual teacher. Pretend they own your business. Act the way they would act.
2. Give gifts, however small, to your customers and employees.
3. Take a walk at lunch.
4. Use a special pen or pencil.
5. Decorate your office or store thematically, according to the time of year.
6. Have fresh flowers on your desk or counter.
7. Bring your pet to work with you when you can.
8. Have contests for your clients/customers/staff.
9. Restructure your day, doing first things last.
10. Surround yourself with pretty objects that make you smile.

11. Light a candle, burn incense, or use an aromatherapy spray.
12. Take regular breaks.
13. Bring puzzles or games and play with them at breaktime.
14. Play upbeat, happy music.
15. Set new goals for yourself and your business.
16. Ask your angels to give you a fun surprise today.
17. When making decisions that affect them, ask your customers for their opinions about your business.
18. Don't take yourself or what you're doing so seriously. Lighten up!
19. Expand what you think is possible for your business. Step outside your comfort zone.
20. Pretend you have amnesia and have lost all your beliefs. Approach everything with a completely open mind.

Try a few of these and see what happens! I am willing to bet you will have more fun which will reflect wonderfully in your business!

Riding the tides of change

No one can escape it these days. Everything is in flux: personal relationships, the weather, politics, and even businesses. Various people I know have shared how some of their cycles and trends have changed, causing them to stand back and shake their heads, wondering what to do.

Today cannot be judged by yesterday. As the many changes are happening, what is critical for us to remember is that our clients and customers are being affected just as much as we are. Just as our needs and desires are shifting, so are theirs. More than ever, it is important to pay attention to our clients in order to find out how we can be of service to them.

Flexibility is one of the most important qualities anyone can develop today. The ability to stay stabilized on shifting sands is admirable – and attainable. Here are some ideas that might help.

- Watch how gracefully nature handles change. She just rolls with it – which holds special meaning for those who felt the recent earthquake in our part of the world. Change is difficult when we refuse to move with it. By taking the time to observe the natural changes around us we can absorb some of nature's ability to adjust quickly and easily.
- Surrender to life; let go of the need to control everything that happens. I admire my dog's ability to do so. I say, "Let's go," and off she runs to the car. When I get up in the morning, she gets up. Bedtime for me is bedtime for her. If I tell her "no," she accepts it without complaining (most of the time). My dog has more trust in me than many of us do in our higher selves or in Spirit. If we truly believe that we are guided and protected by a higher force, let's live that way and surrender ourselves to Spirit's will. A useful mantra for this is "I will to will your will."
- Rediscover the simple joys in life and in your business. Return to the basics. Enjoy breathing, watch the rain fall without judging it, stop to look at all the small flowers growing on weeds you see around you, appreciate every person who calls or drops by your business, and enjoy your talents. Instead of letting change complicate your world, use it as an opportunity to simplify and streamline the way you approach daily life.
- Detach. Detach. Detach. The reason we resist change is that we are far too invested in the way things are or in how we want them to be. Do your best and release the rest. None of us has the ability to see the whole picture – there is always more going on behind the scenes. Make your investment be in the commitment and joy you bring to your work and let the universe take care of the results.
- Don't take yourself or your life personally. Don't let yourself be so serious that you forget to have a good time. Laugh. Joke. Decide to have a good time because of the changes, not in spite of them!
- Experiencing myself as a surfer on the energies of life is very helpful during times of change. My skill comes from being able to stay calm and focused while

moving with the currents of life's waters rather than from trying to make big waves smaller or vice versa. Change is inevitable. Wouldn't life be boring without it?

Today we have the opportunity to become masters of change – let's grasp the chance and see where it takes us!

Success

With every January comes the resolutions and game plan for the next year. How do I want to grow and change? What form of success do I want to have during the next twelve months? Most people spend a lot of time trying to be successful, whether personally or professionally. There is a lot of excellent material available to help us be successful in our businesses as well as in our private lives. However, many of us don't know how to recognize our own successes nor do we know what to expect once we attain our goals.

Because we are naturally oriented to be constantly growing and changing, it is not uncommon for us to work all the way around our successes, not even acknowledging that they have occurred. It is a good idea to take some time on a regular basis and compare where you are today with where you were six months ago, a year ago, and five years ago. It is amazing that we can accomplish so much but get lost in the day-to-day details and not recognize that we have, in fact, succeeded. Instead of trying so hard to *become* a success, we need to focus more of our energy on *enjoying* the success we have already attained.

Take a few moments right now and think of your life five years ago. What did you want then? What was the most important thing you wanted to accomplish? What other goals did you have at the time? How many of these have come to pass – or how many do you no longer care about?

Recently a friend of mine was remembering herself ten years ago when she was just beginning to work after graduating from college. She remembered seeing someone in the grocery store with a twenty dollar bill. "If only I had twenty dollars to spend on groceries," she remembered agonizing to herself. Today she is manifesting $20,000 to pursue her dreams. She is a success - $20 comes easily these days – even while she is pursuing new goals. This is true of all of us if we will only take the time to be grateful for and to enjoy our accomplishments instead of just focusing on whatever it is we are trying to attain.

When we are successful, things happen on both the inner and outer levels. Internally, we'll find ourselves wondering, "What's next?" Which way do I want to grow now? What is my next mountain to climb? Do I want to expand my business or do I want to start something new?

This is perfectly natural and to be expected. When looking at our current level of proficiency, it is a good time to ask ourselves what sort of limits we are setting for ourselves. How high are we willing to go? At what point do we not want to grow any further?

There seems to be an unspoken rule that businesses should always keep expanding. This is not always the case. Sometimes a person reaches a certain level and really doesn't want to take the next step. Because nature won't allow anyone or anything to stand still for any length of time, such an individual would need to look at ways to deepen or enhance what they are currently doing.

For instance, a massage therapist who really doesn't want to enlarge their practice by taking on more clients could enhance their business by learning new forms of body work to offer his or her current clients. A store owner could find new lines of items to carry rather than feeling they have to open a second store. Success demands that we continue to grow in some way. The direction is up to us.

In many cases, though, there will be an internal urge to expand what we're doing and that is when we will need to find out how unlimited we really perceive ourselves to be. Sometimes, we'll try and try to go beyond a certain point only to discover we have some sort of blockage that allows us only so much success and no more. If this happens, it's time for some inner searching and clearing so we can keep progressing the way we feel guided.

Also with success comes new outer circumstances for us to handle. It is not uncommon for successful people to find personal attacks and jealousy coming their way. People who are not living their dreams sometimes lash out and focus their unhappiness on those around them who are successful, when what they really want is to be successful themselves.

Successful people also report they seem to attract people who want to ride on the success of others, want to control them, or who want to be "copy cats." In the alternative spiritual community, one can be open to criticism for not being willing to hand over one's success to others. I will never forget the successful store owner who was approached by more than one person asking for all his wholesale contacts – something it had taken years to develop – so, as the person said, "I can open a store just like yours down the street." The person criticized the store owner for not being willing to "share."

None of these have to be negative experiences, especially if they are seen for what they really are. As we grow, it is natural for us to be placed in situations which will foster further personal development. We are so used to learning through hardship and failure that it can be quite a shock to find out we can learn as much, if not more, from successfully reaching our goals.

If we find ourselves living the success we used to affirm and visualize, we need to realize we are at a new level of understanding and have attained a new ability to manifest on the material plane. Be happy, that means it is time to start a new curriculum!